DATE DUE

AG 18 '94			
OC 21 '94			
DE 9 '94			
AP 19 '96			
SE 25 '96			
AP 7 '98			
AP 28 '98 RENEW			
MY 19 '98			
OC 16 01			

DEMCO 38-296

DARWINISM AND THE AMERICAN INTELLECTUAL
An Anthology

Advisers

David Nasaw
*College of Staten Island
  and the Graduate Center, CUNY*

R. Jackson Wilson
Smith College

AMERICAN SOCIETY AND CULTURE
The Dorsey Collection

DARWINISM AND THE AMERICAN INTELLECTUAL
An Anthology

Second Edition

Edited by
R. Jackson Wilson
Smith College

The Dorsey Press
Chicago, Illinois 60604

© RICHARD D. IRWIN, INC., 1989

Acquisitions editor: Casimir Psujek
Managing editor: Merrily Mazza
Production manager: Ann Cassady
Cover design: Diana Yost
Compositor: Editing, Design & Production, Inc.
Typeface: 10/12 Palatino
Printer: Arcata Graphics/Kingsport

LIBRARY OF CONGRESS
Library of Congress Cataloging-in-Publication Data

Darwinism and the American intellectual : an anthology / edited by R.
  Jackson Wilson. — 2nd ed.
      p.   cm.
    ISBN 0-256-07330-9 (pbk.)
      1. Evolution. 2. Darwin, Charles, 1809–1882. 3. Philosophy,
American. 4. United States—Intellectual life. I. Wilson, Raymond
Jackson.
B818.D27 1989   88–23444
146'.7'0973—dc19   CIP

Printed in the United States of America
1 2 3 4 5 6 7 8 9 0 K 5 4 3 2 1 0 9 8

Table of Contents

CHAPTER 1

Darwinism as
a Scientific Theory

INTRODUCTION

When John Adams was a young schoolmaster, before the American Revolution had begun and forty years before he became the second president of the United States, he kept a diary. There was nothing unusual about this. He had recently graduated from Harvard College, and was teaching school as a way of marking time while he decided whether to become a minister or a lawyer. This was a perfectly conventional thing for a college graduate to do at the time. And it was equally conventional for a young man in his position to keep a journal as record of his daily examinations of himself and his world. All sorts of things went into the diary (a young man could never tell what might turn out to matter). He noted the weather. He kept track of the teas and the dinners he was invited to, and of the conversations he had. He put down his thoughts on the books he read and the sermons he heard. But his purpose went beyond recordkeeping. He was groping for "principles," and the welter of detail in the diary gradually developed a kind of rhythm. Almost daily, he swung between doubt and assurance. He could be sharply critical of himself and the world as he saw it—especially of the way "folly," "passion," and "vice" seemed to control his own and other people's lives. But then he would find comfort in an idea: that God had created an orderly and beneficent world. A young man could hope that through the exercise of reason, he could learn the principles of Divine creation. And if he acted in accord with those principles, he would be part of the grand plan of the world as God had conceived it and brought it forth in the beginning.

Adams' anxieties and hopes no doubt had very personal and private sources. But in his diary he translated the personal and private into categories that were very public. In fact, he made his diary into a kind of morality play, in which whatever was bothering or cheering in his daily life paraded behind masks of abstract ideas about man and nature. On the negative side, he had an ample store of traditional notions about man's frailty and capacity for evil. On the hopeful side, he had confidence in the ultimate reasonableness and goodness of God's government of the world. And so what he weighed in the balance from day to day was not just his or someone else's particular folly or vice, but the principle of evil. And every little victory of daily life was translated into a sign that God had, after all, made the world in ways that a man of reason and virtue could take comfort in. In the end, the pattern that emerged in his diary was one of alternation between experience and design. On the side of experience, the world seemed a place of constant change, disappointment, and ordinary human evil. On the side of design, there was a comforting assurance that the world really was ruled by a changeless, beneficent, and ordered purpose.

John Adams did not invent the notion that the natural world was a product of intelligent and purposeful design. Far from it. The idea belonged to an intellectual tradition that was at least twenty-five centuries old. But more than the weight of tradition was involved. Neither Adams nor any of the countless people who believed in the idea of design kept faith in it because it was consoling, or because it had been sanctified by hundreds of generations of authority, or even because they thought it was implicit in the Old Testament account of the genesis of the world. The concept of design had a tenacious hold because it made a good deal of empirical sense. It rested on three common-sense observations about the way life seemed to work. First, there was an obvious ranking or hierarchy among living things. Some species were obviously "higher" than others—more complicated, perhaps, or, like the Wolf in Little Red Riding Hood, "the better to eat you." As Adams put in his diary, "There is, from the highest species of animals upon this globe, which is generally thought to be man, a regular and uniform subordination of one tribe to another . . . and the same subordination continues quite throughout the vegetable kingdom." Second, this obvious hierarchy was connected to a marvelous and intricate adaptation of living things to their environment and to each other: "If we consider a little of this our globe, we find an endless variety of substances, mutually connected and mutually dependent on each other." Finally, and most important, living things stayed the same forever, reproducing according to their kind. And so all sorts of plants and animals kept their specific place in the order of nature.

"And it is worth observing," as Adams put it, "that each species regularly and uniformly preserves all their [sic] essential and peculiar properties. . . . Every species has its distinguishing properties, and every individual that is born has all those properties without the distinguishing properties of another species."

Here, as Adams and every other educated person knew them, were the facts of life. The world of living things was ordered, its members were exquisitely adapted for success in the niches they occupied, and creatures did not change in their essential characteristics. How could such a marvel be explained? There was only one reasonable hypothesis: an intelligent being must have designed the world, brought it into existence, and sustained its order. "What now," the young Adams asked in triumph, "can preserve this prodigious variety of species, and this inflexible uniformity among the individuals, but the continual and vigilant providence of God."

In John Adams' world, this concept of Providence was utterly conventional. But his diary is an almost perfect example of the way the idea served concrete and very human purposes. Design did, of course, "prove" the existence of God. But it did much more than that. Adams, and thousands of other men and women like him, used the idea to soothe anxieties of every sort, both intellectual and personal. For him, and for most of the other people who used it, the notion of design was an intellectual gesture of consolation for the very present and real troubles and frustrations of life. Design, in other words, was simultaneously a scientific theory, a theological argument, and a comforting moral view. It implied that whatever failures and disappointments might come in experience, life did have meaning. Men and women could hope and believe that their lives and deeds could have moral value if they could be put into harmony with God's (or Nature's) intelligible and purposeful scheme of things.

This way of looking at biology was particularly important at the end of the eighteenth century and the beginning of the nineteenth because of what had been happening in the physical sciences. At the end of the fifteenth century had come Copernicus' argument that the sun, not the earth, was at the center of things. This astonishing idea laid the groundwork for Johannes Kepler's demonstration that the planets kept to orbits that were ellipses, not the circles that educated people had always supposed God had made. Then Galileo showed people that there were mountains on the moon, and that the same laws that governed the behavior of objects on their earth also might explain the behavior of the planets. All this had climaxed at the end of the seventeenth century in the achievements of Isaac Newton, whose work seemed to suggest that there were laws of motion that made the "continual and vigilant providence of God" quite unnecessary to explain the ways physical objects behaved, on earth or in the heavens. As the mystery was taken out of the physical world, the seeming mysteries of the biological world became more and more urgent for those who wanted proof that God not only made things but made them with a purpose, kept them in their place, and continued to govern their actions. For most educated people, the only alternative was to suppose that the world was a moral chaos, and that there were no natural or scientific grounds for believing in any distinction between right and wrong, good and evil.

It was in this cultural situation that Charles Darwin published *On the Origin of Species* (1859). He did not invent the idea of evolution. The possibility that living species appear, change, and disappear had been very much in the air for half a century or so. He did not discover that there was a fossil record that clearly showed that the earth and its creatures were much older than the Bible suggested. This knowledge had become commonplace among educated people during the century before the *Origin of Species*. In fact, for a long time only a minority of intellectually trained men and women had believed that Genesis was more than myth or metaphor. What Darwin did that was challenging was to suggest that it was possible to *explain* the origin of species in a perfectly natural way, and to do so without invoking the idea of an intelligent and purposeful design. He offered an explanation for the most fundamental characteristics of living things that was no more mysterious than the explanations Galileo and Newton had offered for the characteristics of physical objects and their movements. By doing this, Darwin threatened more than a belief in Scripture, more than a scientific hypothesis, more than a theorem in theology. He threatened one of the last great assurances and consolations human beings had that the natural world they were part of was a world of meaning, order, and purpose.

Darwin's explanation of the origin of species was particularly powerful because it actually accepted two of the three main legs on which the idea of design had always stood. There was, he agreed with those who believed in design, a clear hierarchical scheme of relations among species. He was as convinced as any John Adams ever could have been that plant and animal species were astonishingly adapted to their circumstances, clearly "fit" for survival because they were fitted to their place in nature. But Darwin's strategy was to explain these two facts by attacking the third basic principle of the traditional idea of design: that species were fixed, with offspring inheriting the essential characteristics of the species, and passing them along in turn to their offspring. Instead, he proposed that nothing about any species really was essential, but that every characteristic was subject to change. More than this, he argued that it was possible to explain why some of the changes within species turned out to be temporary, while others lasted and became part of the "essential" nature of a new species. This explanation was what he called the theory of natural selection, and it was what was so shattering to people who still clung to traditional ideas of supernatural design.

Darwin did allow that a "Creator" once must have breathed life into the simplest primordial organisms. But from that original mystery forward, in his theory, all living forms had emerged without the assistance of anything supernatural. This meant that the hierarchy and adaptation so central to the theory of design had just *happened*, in the way that other natural events happen. In fact, the existence of higher and lower species, and the fitness of organisms for their place in nature, were both the logical and inevitable outcomes of natural selection. Species had not been created so that they might be nicely subordinated to each other, or suited to their environments. Hierarchy was the outcome of a process of evolutionary branching that had generated new, more complex, and thus higher species, leaving others to occupy their low station in nature. Adaptation was only the result of the fact that every species either accommodates to the changing conditions of life, taking on new characteristics that can be passed from generation to generation, or perishes.

Natural selection was the name Darwin gave to a process that was the result of the joint operation of several different biological facts. Some of these were uncontroversial. The idea that plants and animals generate more offspring than can survive was familiar enough to anyone who had ever puzzled over the curious fact that oaks bear more acorns than could ever become trees, or that any pair of mating animals is likely to produce many more than the two that might replace them. Darwin laboriously made calculations that proved that elephants, the animals with the longest pregnancies, would undergo terrific population explosions unless their numbers were severely checked. The constant threat of overpopulation was not a new idea in Darwin's day. Nor was the second biological fact that he deduced from it: that all living creatures are inevitably engaged in a struggle for survival, a competition that must have more losers than winners. Darwin's scheme also included a third biological fact that seemed obvious and noncontroversial to anyone likely to read his book: that there were individual differences among organisms that made some more likely to survive the struggle than others. The notion that the race is to the swift was hardly news.

It was at this point, though, that Darwin began to part company with traditional wisdom. The traditional concept of species had been that some few defining traits are always passed from parents to offspring, making the species permanent, but that the things that make any individual different are not naturally inherited—*keeping* the species permanent. But suppose, Darwin suggested, that the differences that make one individual more swift than another are not temporary differences that will disappear in the next generation. Suppose that *all* genetic traits are heritable, and not just those that define a species. This would mean that there could be no hard distinction between what was essential to a species and what was temporary and changeable. Further, it would mean that the very idea of species did not refer to a changeless reality. "Species" was an invention of science, used to describe more or less temporary pauses in a natural process whose only reality was change, emergence, development—in a word, evolution. In the struggle for life, poorly adapted individuals tended to die early and have few offspring. These offspring, in their turn, were likely to repeat their parents' unsuccessful careers. Better adapted, more fit individuals lived longer and reproduced more often, and their offspring tended to repeat their successes because they had inherited the variations that had enabled their parents to survive in the first place.

On the Origin of Species was a long and intricate book. But it was carefully framed around its central argument, that the arduous process of natural selection, working over almost incalculable stretches of geological time, could have produced every form of life known in nature and in the fossil record. Natural selection, the *Origin* also argued, could have produced the family resemblances and the hierarchy among different species. Natural selection could explain why every living thing seemed so marvelously equipped to survive in its environment and to reproduce offspring that could do the same.

Darwin's theory had some important advantages over the idea that every species had been specially created to fill its place in the world's design. The *Origin* was, on the whole, a scientific work. Its only concession to the supernatural was to say that God had been responsible for the very beginnings of life. Darwin was proposing to expand the scope of natural science to include more phenomena, and this put his work into the favoring currents of the long scientific revolution that had been the most potent intellectual development in Western society for the preceding four centuries. Darwin's theory explained a number of facts of nature—resemblances between species, for example—that had always been referred to the symmetrical will (or doggedness, perhaps) of a Creator. On the theory of natural selection, it finally made sense that mammals of different species should have similar hearts, or that there should be striking skeletal similarities among all the vertebrates. It was not that God, having figured out how to make a heart or a spinal column, decided to stick with a design that worked. Mammals were related, not just structurally but genealogically. Vertebrates, too—snakes, birds, cows and the like—had certain likenesses because they were all distant evolutionary cousins. For the defenders of Darwin, in America and everywhere else, the naturalistic and explanatory power of the theory of evolution were its greatest attraction and advantage.

This did not mean, though, that the scientific truth of the theory was self-evident. Theories can be powerful and still not be true, and Darwin's conception had enough problems to make it possible for men or women to reject it—and not just because it ran counter to a literal reading of Genesis. There were scientists and philosophers of impressive learning and ability who could build an anti-Darwinian case on reasonable and apparently scientific objections. For one thing, Darwin could not identify the *cause* of variation, and this made it impossible for him to produce any real proof that variations could be inherited. Darwin did point to the successful breeding of domestic animals. But his opponents could argue that breeding created new varieties, not new species, and that domesticated varieties never maintained their characteristics for long in untended, natural settings.

The thinness of the fossil record also embarrassed Darwin and his followers. There were large numbers of fossil species for which preceding rock strata showed no long, slow, cumulative preparation. Many, perhaps even most, species seemed simply to spring to life fully grown at the dawn of a particular geological age. They then persisted through their age (as defined by the rocks) without changing, then disappeared without an evolutionary trace. The fossil record had been produced by an effect something like a great strobe light that reveals a long but frozen evolutionary moment, then shuts off

SOLACE - COMFORT.

for a period of darkness in which nothing is recorded, then comes on again to capture another evolutionary moment. The very reason that the rocks *have* strata is that they are radically discontinuous. As a result, countless numbers of forms that must have intervened between known and related species are simply missing from the fossil record. Darwin asked his readers for an act of faith almost as profound as a faith in creation: to believe that what was missing from the rocks had really once lived and bred. His critics understood perfectly well that this was one of the vulnerable points of the *Origin*.

Worst of all, perhaps, was the fact that Darwin could account for the gradual improvement of special organs like the eye, but had difficulty explaining their beginnings. Presumably, the rudimentary beginnings of an eye would have had no survival value. Indeed, creatures with such a useless and perhaps irritating warp of tissue might have been worse off in evolutionary terms.

For these and other similar reasons, it was perfectly possible for scientists and sophisticated intellectuals of quite sound mind to refuse to accept the hypothesis of natural selection. Darwin's most formidable scientific opponent in the United States was Harvard zoologist Louis Agassiz (1807–1873), a naturalized Swiss who had already achieved a very high reputation in Europe before he came to the United States in 1846. By the time of the publication of the *Origin*, Agassiz had more prestige—and even popularity—than any other scientist in America. His opposition to Darwin became the most important solace for other American opponents of evolution, especially for nonscientists who attacked Darwin for religious reasons. (The selection printed here is from the third volume of Agassiz's *Contributions to the Natural History of the United States*. The *American Journal of Science and Arts* excerpted it from advance proof sheets of the *Contributions* and printed it in 1860 as Agassiz's review of Darwin's *Origin of Species*.)

Agassiz dismissed the *Origin* as a collection of "marvellous bear, cuckoo, and other stories"—as just another example of the credulous tales, fables and speculations that had plagued botany and zoology for many centuries. This was not so absurd in 1860 as it might seem today. For if the *Origin* was fundamentally a scientific book, it was still a very speculative book. It was heavy with observations of fact. But at crucial theoretical points, Darwin was reduced to such groping expressions as "not improbably" or "not impossible." Occasionally, Darwin even introduced what he called "imaginary" examples. In the end, it was not the weight of Darwin's empirical evidence but the intellectual structure of his theory that

GROPING - SEARCH FOR BY FEELING.

was scientific. The concept of design had always been an overt confession of the inability of science to account for such basic phenomena as species, resemblance, and adaptation. Whatever might be its shortages of evidence, Darwin's theory at least pointed in scientific directions. This was what made it possible for other scientists, after 1860, to begin to produce new evidence—and made it a practical certainty as well that evolution would become scientific orthodoxy before a generation had passed.

Agassiz offered as his alternative to evolution his own theory of sequential creation—a theory that put as heavy a strain on faith as the six days of Genesis. At the end of each geological period (marked by the separations between rock and fossil strata), the Creator had wiped the slate of life clean and created a set of new species. These might resemble the species of the preceding geological age. But the resemblance was between the *ideas* of species in the Creative Mind, not a resemblance between biological ancestors and their descendants. Agassiz's concept of sequential special creation was not really an attempt to explain what was in the rocks, but the radical discontinuities between what was in one layer of rock and what was in the layer just above it.

What Agassiz was really defending, though, was not a Biblical notion of creation but philosophical idealism. He was convinced that reality belongs not to concrete and material things but to ideas, and not to people's ideas, either, but to Ideas that transcend the world of things and people, and indeed make that world possible. Species, Agassiz argued, were like all other facts of nature: they were the products of thoughts in the mind of God. And science could only be a kind of divine psychology, whose purpose was to show that God did not think about one thing at a time, but thought in categories like species, and in hierarchies of categories, like the biologists' families and genera. He needed a good many capital letters to describe this conception of inquiry: "The Study of Nature is intercourse with the Highest Mind." No amount of scientific observation or experiment could confirm such a philosophical position—or disprove it, either. The conceptual choice Agassiz was posing was not just a choice between evolution and creation. It was a choice between ways of thinking that could be subjected to tests of evidence and others that could not be. It was at least possible to look at a bit of evidence—a bone, for example, or a fossilized fish—and say, "This appears to add weight to the idea of natural selection," or "It would seem that this new object makes it less likely that natural selection explains the origin of species." Strategically, if men and women decided to choose such a conception of science (as against "intercourse with the Highest Mind") they had to choose some version of evolution, since it was the only scientific hypothesis in the field. It was only a matter of time, and a quite brief time at that, until scientists and intellectuals (including Agassiz's friends and his own son) adopted the evolutionary alternative.

Agassiz's principal opponent was his Harvard colleague, the botanist Asa Gray (1810–1888). Gray was the most active and prolific of pro-Darwinian scientists in the United States. His initial review of the *Origin*, which also appeared in the *American Journal of Science and Arts*, is included in this chapter. The review is a fine illustration of the fact that in 1860 even the most serious professional scientist could not regard the *Origin* as a purely scientific work. Darwin himself was agitated by the philosophical and religious implications of his theory. And Gray could not ignore these implications, even though his review was in a scientific journal intended mainly for an audience of fellow scientists. At the close of the review, Gray claimed that evolution still implied a "Divinity that shapes these ends." In an essay written a few months later for a more popular magazine, Gray even argued that man, unlike all the lower species, had been privileged to a special and miraculous creation. Gray was not merely indulging in a careful "soft sell" of Darwinism. He was attempting to save the consolatory and religious advantages of design for the theory of evolution, to suggest to moralists and theologians that the Darwinian theory might be regarded as a new appendix to Scripture. From evolution, he hoped, it might be possible to draw just as potent a revelation of God's operations as had been available in the older idea of the permanence of species.

PROFESSOR AGASSIZ ON THE ORIGIN OF SPECIES*

Louis Agassiz

A few years ago the prevailing opinion among naturalists was that, while genera, families, orders, classes, and any other more or less

---

*From the *American Journal of Science and Arts*, Second Series, 30 (1860), pp. 142–54.

comprehensive divisions among animals were artificial devices of science to facilitate our studies, species alone had a real existence in nature. . . . Darwin's fundamental idea, on the contrary, is that species, genera, families, orders, classes, and any other kind of more or less comprehensive divisions among animals do not exist at all, and are altogether artificial, differing from one another only in degree, all having originated from a successive differentiation of a primordial organic form, undergoing successively such changes as would at first produce a variety of species; then genera, as the difference became more extensive and deeper; then families, as the gap widened still farther between the groups, until in the end all that diversity was produced which has existed or exists now. Far from agreeing with these views, I have, on the contrary, taken the ground that all the natural divisions in the animal kingdom are primarily distinct, founded upon different categories of characters, and that all exist in the same way, that is, as categories of thought, embodied in individual living forms. . . .

Since the arguments presented by Darwin in favor of a universal derivation from one primary form, of all the peculiarities existing now among living beings have not made the slightest impression on my mind, nor modified in any way the views I have already propounded, . . . I will here only add a single argument, which seems to leave the question where I have placed it.

It seems to me that there is much confusion of ideas in the general statement of the variability of species so often repeated lately. If species do not exist at all, as the supporters of the transmutation theory maintain, how can they vary? and if individuals alone exist, how can the differences which may be observed among them prove the variability of species? The fact seems to me to be that while species are based upon definite relations among individuals which differ in various ways among themselves, each individual, as a distinct being, has a definite course to run from the time of its first formation to the end of its existence, during which it never loses its identity nor changes its individuality, nor its relations to other individuals belonging to the same species, but preserves all the categories of relationship which constitute specific or generic or family affinity, or any other kind or degree of affinity. *To prove that species vary it should be proved that individuals born from common ancestors change the different categories of relationship which they bore primitively to one another.* While all that has thus far been shown is, that there exists a considerable difference among individuals of one and the same species. . . . But as long as no fact is adduced to show that any one well known species among the many thousands that are buried in the whole series of fossiliferous rocks, is actually the parent of any one of the species now living, such arguments can have no weight; and thus far the supporters of the transmutation theory have failed to produce any such facts. Instead of facts we are treated with marvelous bear, cuckoo, and other stories. . . .

Had Mr. Darwin or his followers furnished a single fact to show that individuals change, in the course of time, in such a manner as to produce at last species different from those known before, the state of the case might be different. But it stands recorded now as before, that the animals known to the ancients are still in existence, exhibiting to this day the characters they exhibited of old. The geological record, even with all its imperfections, exaggerated to distortion, tells now, what it has told from the beginning, that the supposed intermediate forms between the species of different geological periods are imaginary beings, called up merely in support of a fanciful theory. The origin of all the diversity among living beings remains a mystery as totally unexplained as if the book of Mr. Darwin had never been written, for no theory unsupported by fact, however plausible it may appear, can be admitted in science.

It seems generally admitted that the work of Darwin is particularly remarkable for the fairness with which he presents the facts adverse to his views. It may be so; but I confess that it has made a very different impression upon me. I have been more forcibly struck by his inability to perceive when the facts are fatal to his argument, than by anything else in the whole book. His chapter on the Geological Record, in particular, appears to me, from beginning to end, as a series of illogical deductions and misrepresentations of the modern results of Geology and Palaeontology. I do not intend to argue here, one by one, the questions he has discussed. Such arguments end too often in special pleading, and any one familiar with the subject may readily perceive where the truth lies by confronting his assertions with the geological record itself. But since the question at issue is chiefly to be settled by palaeontological evidence, and I have devoted the greater part of my life to the special study of the fossils, I wish to record my protest against his mode of treating this part of the subject. Not only does Darwin never perceive when the facts are fatal to his views, but when he has succeeded by an ingenious circumlocution in overleaping the facts, he would have us believe that he has lessened their importance or changed their meaning. He would thus have us believe that there have been periods during which all that had taken place during other periods was destroyed, and this solely to explain the absence of intermediate forms between the fossils found in successive deposits, for the origin of which he looks to those missing links; whilst every recent progress in Geology shows more and more fully how gradual and successive all the deposits have been which form the crust of our earth.

He would have us believe that entire faunae have disappeared before those were preserved, the remains of which are found in the lowest fossiliferous strata; when we find everywhere non-fossiliferous strata below those that contain the oldest fossils now known. It is true, he explains their absence by the supposition that they were too delicate to be preserved; but any animals from which Crinoids, Brachiopods, Cephalopods, and Trilobites could arise, must have been sufficiently similar to them to have left, at least, traces of their presence in the lowest non-fossiliferous rocks, had they ever existed at all.* He would have us believe that the oldest organisms that existed were simple cells, or something like the lowest living beings now in existence; when such highly organized animals as Trilobites and Orthoceratites** are among the oldest known. He would have us believe that these lowest first-born became extinct in consequence of the gradual advantage some of their more favored descendants gained over the majority of their predecessors; when there exist now, and have existed at all periods in past history, as large a proportion of more simply organized beings, as of more favored types, and when such types as Lingula were among the lowest Silurian fossils, and are alive at the present

---

*[Editor's note: Crinoids, brachiopods, cephalopods and trilobites were all marine animals which were very widespread during the first geological period for which there is any appreciable fossil record. The problem Agassiz raised here was one of the most nagging difficulties with which Darwinists had to contend. All the strata known as Cambrian, which are about 500,000,000 years old, contained fossils of complex animals, but in the rocks just below, there were no fossil remains of forms leading up to such complicated and articulated organisms as the trilobite.]

**[Editor's note: Orthoceratites, like trilobites, were an extinct marine animal whose fossils were present in Cambrian rock.]

day.* He would have us believe that each new species originated in consequence of some slight change in those that preceded; when every geological formation teems with types that did not exist before. He would have us believe that animals and plants became gradually more and more numerous; when most species appear in myriads of individuals, in the first bed in which they are found. He would have us believe that animals disappear gradually; when they are as common in the uppermost bed in which they occur as in the lowest, or any intermediate bed. Species appear suddenly and disappear suddenly in successive strata. That is the fact proclaimed by Palaeontology; they neither increase successively in number, nor do they gradually dwindle down; none of the fossil remains thus far observed show signs of a gradual improvement or of a slow decay. . . .

He would also have us believe that the most perfect organs of the body of animals are the product of gradual improvement, when eyes as perfect as those of the Trilobites are preserved with the remains of these oldest animals. He would have us believe that it required millions of years to effect any one of these changes; when far more extraordinary transformations are daily going on, under our eyes, in the shortest periods of time, during the growth of animals. He would have us believe that animals acquire their instincts gradually; when even those that never see their parents, perform at birth the same acts, in the same way, as their progenitors. He would have us believe that the geographical distribution of animals is the result of accidental transfers; when most species are so narrowly confined within the limits of their natural range, that even slight changes in their external relations may cause their death. And all these, and many other calls upon our credulity, are coolly made in the face of an amount of precise information, readily accessible, which would overwhelm any one who does not place his opinions above the records of an age eminently characterized for its industry, and during which, that information was laboriously accumulated by crowds of faithful laborers.

It would be superfluous to discuss in detail the arguments by which Mr. Darwin attempts to explain the diversity among animals. Suffice it to say, that he has lost sight of the most striking of the fea-

---

*[Editor's note: Lingula was a burrowing, clam-like animal which still existed, apparently unchanged since its fossil remains were deposited in the Silurian period, one of the oldest of fossil strata.]

tures, and the one which pervades the whole, namely, that there runs throughout Nature unmistakable evidence of thought, corresponding to the mental operations of our own mind, and therefore intelligible to us as thinking beings, and unaccountable on any other basis than that they owe their existence to the working of intelligence; and no theory that overlooks this element can be true to nature.

There are naturalists who seem to look upon the idea of creation, that is, a manifestation of an intellectual power by material means, as a kind of bigotry; forgetting, no doubt, that whenever they carry out a thought of their own, they do something akin to creating, unless they look upon their own elucubrations as something in which their individuality is not concerned, but arising without an intervention of their mind, in consequence of the working of some "bundles of forces," about which they know nothing themselves. And yet such men are ready to admit that matter is omnipotent, and consider a disbelief in the omnipotence of matter as tantamount to imbecility; for, what is the assumed power of matter to produce all finite beings, but omnipotence? And what is the outcry raised against those who cannot admit it, but an insinuation that they are *non-compos*? The book of Mr. Darwin is free of all such uncharitable sentiments towards his fellow-laborers in the field of science; nevertheless his mistake lies in a similar assumption that the most complicated system of combined thoughts can be the result of accidental causes; for he ought to know, as every physicist will concede, that all the influences to which he would ascribe the origin of species are accidental in their very nature, and he must know, as every naturalist familiar with the modern progress of science does know, that the organized beings which live now, and have lived in former geological periods, constitute an organic whole, intelligibly and methodically combined in all its parts. . . .

The fallacy of Mr. Darwin's theory of the origin of species by means of natural selection may be traced in the first few pages of his book, where he overlooks the difference between the voluntary and deliberate acts of selection applied methodically by man to the breeding of domesticated animals and the growing of cultivated plants, and the chance influences which may affect animals and plants in the state of nature. To call these influences "natural selection," is a misnomer which will not alter the conditions under which they may produce the desired results. Selection implies design; the powers to which Darwin refers the order of species, can design nothing. Selection is no doubt the essential principle on which the raising of breeds is founded, and the subject of breeds is presented in its true light by Mr. Darwin; but this process of raising breeds by the selection of favorable subjects, is in no way similar to that which regulates specific differences. Nothing is more remote from the truth than the attempted parallelism between the breeds of domesticated animals and the species of wild ones. . . .

All attempts to explain the origin of species may be brought under two categories: viz. 1st, some naturalists admitting that all organized beings are created, that is to say, endowed from the beginning of their existence with all their characteristics, while 2d, others assume that they arise spontaneously. This classification of the different theories of the origin of species, may appear objectionable to the supporters of the transmutation theory; but I can perceive no essential difference between their views and the old idea that animals may have arisen spontaneously. They differ only in the modes by which the spontaneous appearance is assumed to be effected. . . . I believe these theories will, in the end, all share the fate of the theory of spontaneous generations so called, as the facts of nature shall be confronted more closely with the theoretical assumptions. . . . Unless Darwin and his followers succeed in showing that the struggle for life tends to something beyond favoring the existence of certain individuals over that of other individuals, they will soon find that they are following a shadow. The assertion of Darwin, which has crept into the title of his work, is, that favored *races* are preserved, while all his facts go only to substantiate the assertion, that favored *individuals* have a better chance in the struggle for life than others. But who has ever overlooked the fact that myriads of individuals of every species constantly die before coming to maturity? What ought to be shown, if the transmutation theory is to stand, is that these favored individuals diverge from their specific type, and neither Darwin nor any body else has furnished a single fact to show that they go on diverging. The criterion of a true theory consists in the facility with which it accounts for facts accumulated in the course of long-continued investigations and for which the existing theories afforded no explanation. It can certainly not be said that Darwin's theory will stand by that test. . . .

Whatever views are correct concerning the origin of the species, one thing is certain, that as long as they exist they continue to produce generation after generation, individuals which differ from one another only in such peculiarities as relate to their individuality. . . . Whatever minor differences may exist between the products of this succession of generations are all *individual peculiarities*, in no way connected with the essential features of the species, and therefore as transient as the individuals; while the specific characters are forever fixed. . . .

Let it not be objected that the individuals of successive generations have presented marked differences among themselves; for these differences, with all the monstrosities that may have occurred, during these countless generations, have passed away with the individuals, as individual peculiarities, and the specific characteristics alone have been preserved, together with all that distinguishes the genus, the family, the order, the class, and the branch to which the individual belonged. Moreover all this has been maintained through a succession of repeated changes, amounting in each individual to the whole range of transformations, through which an individual passes, from the time it is individualized as an egg, to the time it is itself capable of reproducing its kind, and, perhaps, with all the intervening phases of an unequal production of males and females, of sterile individuals, of dwarfs, of giants, etc., etc., during which there were millions of chances for a deviation from the type. Does this not prove that while individuals are perishable, they transmit, generation after generation, all that is specific or generic, or, in one word, *typical* in them, to the exclusion of every *individual peculiarity* which passes away with them, and that, therefore, while individuals alone have a material existence, species, genera, families, orders, classes, and branches of the animal kingdom exist only as categories of thought in the Supreme Intelligence, but as such have as truly an independent existence and are as unvarying as thought itself after it has once been expressed. . . .

Were the transmutation theory true, the geological record should exhibit an uninterrupted succession of types blending gradually into one another. The fact is that throughout all geological times each period is characterized by definite specific types, belonging to definite genera, and these to definite families, referable to definite orders, constituting definite classes and definite branches, built upon definite plans. Until the facts of Nature are shown to have been mistaken by those who have collected them, and that they have a different meaning from that now generally assigned to them, I shall therefore consider the transmutation theory as a scientific mistake, untrue in its facts, unscientific in its method, and mischievous in its tendency.

PERUSAL- READ ATTENTIVELY.

REVIEW OF DARWIN'S THEORY ON
THE ORIGIN OF SPECIES*

Asa Gray

This book is already exciting much attention. Two American editions are announced, through which it will become familiar to many of our readers, before these pages are issued. . . . Who, upon a single perusal, shall pass judgment upon a work like this, to which twenty of the best years of the life of a most able naturalist have been devoted? And who among those naturalists who hold a position that entitles them to pronounce summarily upon the subject, can be expected to divest himself for the nonce of the influence of received and favorite systems? In fact, the controversy now opened is not likely to be settled in an off-hand way, nor is it desirable that it should be. A spirited conflict among opinions of every grade must ensue, which,—to borrow an illustration from the doctrine of the book before us—may be likened to the conflict in nature among races in the struggle for life, which Mr. Darwin describes; through which the views most favored by facts will be developed and tested by 'Natural Selection,' the weaker ones be destroyed in the process, and the strongest in the long run alone survive. . . .

That the existing kinds of animals and plants, or many of them, may be derived from other and earlier kinds, in the lapse of time, is by no means a novel proposition. Not to speak of ancient speculations of the sort, it is the well-known Lamarckian theory.** The first difficulty which such theories meet with is that, in the

---

*From the *American Journal of Science and Arts*, Second Series, 29 (1860), pp. 153–84.

**[Editor's note: Jean Baptiste Lamarck (1744–1829) was a French zoologist who was the first partisan of evolution in its modern form. Lamarck's *Philosophie Zoologique* (1809) argued that species evolved because changes in an organism during its lifetime were transmitted to its offspring. These changes, according to Lamarck, resulted primarily from the influences of the environment, such as climate, and from habits of use and disuse. For example, living in a sunny climate might make a man's skin darker, in which case his children would be born with dark skin, so that eventually a black-skinned race would evolve. Or, living in an area where food was scarce, an animal might strain to reach leaves higher and higher on bushes and trees. In the long run, an animal like the giraffe would result from such habitual use of the neck. Darwin, on the contrary, believed that the variations which caused evolution were tied entirely to the reproductive process, and not to changes occurring during the lifetime of an organism, though in successive editions of the *Origin* Darwin made some concessions to the Lamarckian theory.]

present age, with all its own and its inherited prejudgments, the whole burden of proof is naturally, and indeed properly, laid upon the shoulders of the propounders; and thus far the burden has been more than they could bear. From the very nature of the case, substantive proof of specific creation is not attainable; but that of derivation or transmutation of species may be. He who affirms the latter view is bound to do one or both of two things. Either, 1, to assign real and adequate causes, the natural or necessary result of which must be to produce the present diversity of species and their actual relations; or, 2, to show the general conformity of the whole body of facts to such assumption, and also to adduce instances explicable by it and inexplicable by the received view,—so perhaps winning our assent to the doctrine, through its competency to harmonize all the facts, even though the cause of the assumed variation remain as occult as that of the transformation of tadpoles into frogs. . . .

The first line of proof, successfully carried out, would establish derivation as a true physical theory; the second, as a sufficient hypothesis.

Lamarck mainly undertook the first line, in a theory which has been so assailed by ridicule that it rarely receives the credit for ability to which in its day it was entitled. But he assigned partly unreal, partly insufficient causes; and the attempt to account for a progressive change in species through the direct influence of physical agencies, and through the appetencies and habits of animals reacting upon their structure, thus causing the production and the successive modification of organs, is a conceded and total failure. The shadowy author of the Vestiges of the Natural History of Creation* can hardly be said to have undertaken either line, in a scientific way. He would explain the whole progressive evolution of nature by virtue of an inherent tendency to development,—thus giving us an idea or a word in place of a natural cause, a restatement of the proposition instead of an explanation. Mr. Darwin attempts both lines of proof, and in a strictly scientific spirit; but the stress falls mainly upon the first; for, as he does assign real causes, he is bound to prove their adequacy.

It should be kept in mind that, while all direct proof of independent origination is unattainable from the nature of the case, the

---

*[Editor's note: Vestiges of the Natural History of Creation was published anonymously in 1844 by a Scot, Robert Chambers (1802–1871). It was a nonscientific attempt to remove religious objections to the idea of evolution.]

overthrow of particular schemes of derivation has not established the opposite proposition. The futility of each hypothesis thus far proposed to account for derivation may be made apparent, or unanswerable objections may be urged against it; and each victory of the kind may render derivation more improbable, and therefore specific creation more probable, without settling the question either way. New facts, or new arguments and a new mode of viewing the question may some day change the whole aspect of the case. It is with the latter that Mr. Darwin now reopens the discussion.

Having conceived the idea that varieties are incipient species, he is led to study variation in the field where it shows itself most strikingly and affords the greatest facilities to investigation. Thoughtful naturalists have had increasing grounds to suspect that a re-examination of the question of species in zoology and botany, commencing with those races which man knows most about, viz. the domesticated and cultivated races, would be likely somewhat to modify the received idea of the entire fixity of species. This field, rich with various but unsystematized stores of knowledge accumulated by cultivators and breeders, has been generally neglected by naturalists, because these races are not in a state of nature; whereas they deserve particular attention on this very account, as experiments, or the materials for experiments, ready to our hand. In domestication we vary some of the natural conditions of a species, and thus learn experimentally what changes are within the reach of varying conditions in nature. We separate and protect a favorite race against its foes or its competitors, and thus learn what it might become if nature ever afforded it equal opportunities. Even when, to subserve human uses, we modify a domesticated race to the detriment of its native vigor, or to the extent of practical monstrosity, although we secure forms which would not be originated and could not be perpetuated in free nature, yet we attain wider and juster views of the possible degree of variation. We perceive that some species are more variable than others, but that no species subjected to the experiment persistently refuses to vary; and that when it has once begun to vary, its varieties are not the less but the more subject to variation. "No case is on record of a variable being ceasing to be variable under cultivation." It is fair to conclude, from the observation of plants and animals in a wild as well as domesticated state, that the tendency to vary is general, and even universal. Mr. Darwin does "not believe that variability is an inherent and necessary contingency, under all circumstances, with all organic beings, as some authors have thought." No one supposes variation could occur under all circumstances; but the facts on the whole imply an universal tendency, ready to be manifested under favorable circumstances. . . .

The actual causes of variation are unknown. . . . Really, we no more know the reason why the progeny occasionally deviates from the parent than we do why it usually resembles it. Though the laws and conditions governing variation are known to a certain extent, while those governing inheritance are apparently inscrutable. "Perhaps," Darwin remarks, "the correct way of viewing the whole subject would be, to look at the inheritance of every character whatever as the rule, and non-inheritance as the anomaly." This, from general and obvious considerations, we have long been accustomed to do. Now, as exceptional instances are expected to be capable of explanation, while ultimate laws are not, it is quite possible that variation may be accounted for, while the great primary law of inheritance remains a mysterious fact.

The common proposition is, that *species reproduce their like;* this is a sort of general inference, only to a degree closer to fact than the statement that genera reproduce their like. The true proposition, the fact incapable of further analysis is, that *individuals reproduce their like,* —that characteristics are inheritable. So varieties, or deviations once originated, are perpetuable, like species. . . .

In this way races arise, which under favorable conditions may be as hereditary as species. In following these indications, watching opportunities, and breeding only from those individuals which vary most in a desirable direction, man leads the course of variation as he leads a streamlet,—apparently at will, but never against the force of gravitation,—to a long distance from its source, and makes it more subservient to his use or fancy. He unconsciously strengthens those variations which he prizes when he plants the seed of a favorite fruit, preserves a favorite domestic animal, drowns the uglier kittens of a litter, and allows only the handsomest or the best mousers to propagate. Still more, by methodical selection, in recent times almost marvellous results have been produced in new breeds of cattle, sheep, and poultry, and new varieties of fruit of greater and greater size or excellence. . . .

We see everywhere around us the remarkable results which Nature may be said to have brought about under artificial selection and separation. Could she accomplish similar results when left to herself? Variations might begin, we know they do begin, in a wild state. But would any of them be preserved and carried to an equal degree of deviation? Is there anything in nature which in the long run may answer to artificial selection? Mr. Darwin thinks that there is; and *Natural Selection* is the key-note of his discourse.

As a preliminary, he has a short chapter to show that there is variation in nature, and therefore something for natural selection to act upon. He readily shows that such mere variations as may be directly referred to physical conditions (like the depauperation of plants in a sterile soil, or their dwarfing as they approach an alpine summit, the thicker fur of an animal from far northward, &c.), and also those individual differences which we everywhere recognize but do not pretend to account for, are not separable by any assignable line from more strongly marked varieties; likewise that there is no clear demarcation between the latter and subspecies, or varieties of the highest grade (distinguished from species not by any known inconstancy, but by the supposed lower importance of their characteristics); nor between these and recognized species. "These differences blend into each other in an insensible series, and the series impresses the mind with an idea of an actual passage." . . .

In applying his principle of natural selection to the work in hand, Mr. Darwin assumes, as we have seen: 1, some variability of animals and plants in nature; 2, the absence of any definite distinction between slight variations, and varieties of the highest grade; 3, the fact that naturalists do not practically agree, and do not increasingly tend to agree, as to what forms are species and what are strong varieties, thus rendering it probable that there may be no essential and original difference, or no possibility of ascertaining it, at least in many cases; also, 4, that the most flourishing and dominant species of the larger genera on an average vary most . . . and, 5, that in large genera the species are apt to be closely but unequally allied together, forming little clusters round certain species,—just such clusters as would be formed if we suppose their members once to have been satellites or varieties of a central or parent species, but to have attained at length a wider divergence and a specific character. The fact of such association is undeniable; and the use which Mr. Darwin makes of it seems fair and natural.

The gist of Mr. Darwin's work is to show that such varieties are gradually diverged into species and genera through *natural selection;* that natural selection is the inevitable result of the *struggle for existence* which all living things are engaged in; and that this struggle is an unavoidable consequence of several natural causes, but mainly of the high rate at which all organic beings tend to increase.

Curiously enough, Mr. Darwin's theory is grounded upon the

doctrine of Malthus and the doctrine of Hobbes.* The elder DeCandolle had conceived the idea of the struggle for existence, and in a passage which would have delighted the cynical philosopher of Malmesbury, had declared that all nature is at war, one organism with another or with external nature; and Lyell and Herbert had made considerable use of it.** But Hobbes in his theory of society and Darwin in his theory of natural history, alone have built their systems upon it. However moralists and political economists may regard these doctrines in their original application to human society and the relation of population to subsistence, their thorough applicability to the great society of the organic world in general is now undeniable. And to Mr. Darwin belongs the credit of making this extended application, and of working out the immensely diversified results with rare sagacity and untiring patience. He has brought to view *real causes* which have been largely operative in the establishment of the actual association and geographical distribution of plants and animals. In this he must be allowed to have made a very important contribution to an interesting department of science, even if his theory fails in the endeavor to explain the origin or diversity of species. . . .

The interest for the general reader heightens as the author advances on his perilous way and grapples manfully with the most formidable difficulties.

To account, upon these principles, for the gradual elimination and segregation of nearly allied forms,—such as varieties, subspecies, and closely related or representative species,—also in a general way for their geographical association and present range, is comparatively easy, is apparently within the bounds of possibility, and even of probability. Could we stop here we should be fairly contented. But, to complete the system, to carry out the principles

---

*[Editor's note: Thomas Malthus (1766–1834) was the author of *Essay on the Principle of Population* (1798), which argued that populations always expand to the limit of the means of subsistence, thus causing a "struggle for existence." Thomas Hobbes (1588–1679), the "cynical philosopher of Malmesbury," was the author of *Leviathan* (1651), an egoistic ethics which also emphasized the struggle for survival.]

**[Editor's note: Pyrame de Candolle (1778–1841) was a Swiss botanist who proposed a system of animal classification based on an evolutionary conception of species. Sir Charles Lyell (1797–1875) wrote the most authoritative geological text of the 19th century, the *Principles of Geology* (1830–1833), which helped lay the groundwork for Darwin's theory. Edmond Herbert (1812–1890) was a French geologist who also helped prepare the way for the *Origin* by his work on fossils in chalk deposits.]

to their ultimate conclusion, and to explain by them many facts in geographical distribution which would still remain anomalous, Mr. Darwin is equally bound to account for the formation of genera, families, orders, and even classes, by natural selection. He does "not doubt that the theory of descent with modification embraces all the members of the same class," and he concedes that analogy would press the conclusion still farther; while he admits that "the more distinct the forms are, the more the arguments fall away in force." To command assent we naturally require decreasing probability to be overbalanced by an increased weight of evidence. An opponent might plausibly, and perhaps quite fairly, urge that the links in the chain of argument are weakest just where the greatest stress falls upon them.

To which Mr. Darwin's answer is, that the best parts of the testimony have been lost. He is confident that intermediate forms must have existed; that in the olden times when the genera, the families and the orders diverged from their parent stocks, gradations existed as fine as those which now connect closely related species with varieties. But they have passed and left no sign. The geological record, even if all displayed to view, is a book from which not only many pages, but even whole alternate chapters have been lost out, or rather which were never printed from the autographs of nature. The record was actually made in fossil lithography only at certain times and under certain conditions (i.e., at periods of slow subsidence and places of abundant sediment); and of these records all but the last volume is out of print; and of its pages only local glimpses have been obtained. Geologists, except Lyell, will object to this,—some of them moderately, others with vehemence. Mr. Darwin himself admits, with a candor rarely displayed on such occasions, that he should have expected more geological evidence of transition than he finds, and that all the most eminent palæontologists maintain the immutability of species.

The general fact, however, that the fossil fauna of each period as a whole is nearly intermediate in character between the preceding and the succeeding faunas, is much relied on. We are brought one step nearer to the desired inference by the similar "fact, insisted on by all palaeontologists, that fossils from two consecutive formations are far more closely related to each other, than are the fossils of two remote formations. . . . "

We pass to a second difficulty in the way of Mr. Darwin's theory; to a case where we are perhaps entitled to demand of him evidence of gradation. . . . Wide, very wide is the gap, anatomically and physiologically (we do not speak of the intellectual) between the highest quadrumana and man; and comparatively recent, if ever, must the line have bifurcated. But where is there the slightest evidence of a common progenitor? Perhaps Mr. Darwin would reply by another question: where are the fossil remains of the men who made the flint knives and arrow-heads of the Somme valley?

A fourth* and the most formidable difficulty is that of the production and specialization of organs.

It is well said that all organic beings have been formed on two great laws; Unity of type, and Adaptation to the conditions of existence. . . . Philosophical minds form various conceptions for harmonizing the two views theoretically. Mr. Darwin harmonizes and explains them naturally. Adaptation to the conditions of existence is the result of Natural Selection; Unity of type, of unity of descent. Accordingly, as he puts his theory, he is bound to account for the origination of new organs, and for their diversity in each great type, for their specialization, and every adaptation of organ to function and of structure to condition, through natural agencies. Whenever he attempts this he reminds us of Lamarck, and shows us how little light the science of a century devoted to structural investigation has thrown upon the mystery of organization. Here purely natural explanations fail. The organs being given, natural selection may account for some improvement; if given of a variety of sorts or grades, natural selection might determine which should survive and where it should prevail.

On all this ground the only line for the theory to take is to make the most of gradation and adherence to type as suggestive of derivation, and unaccountable upon any other scientific view, —deferring all attempts to explain *how* such a metamorphosis was effected, until naturalists have explained *how* the tadpole is metamorphosed into a frog, or one sort of polyp into another. As to *why* it is so, the philosophy of efficient cause, and even the whole argument from design, would stand, upon the admission of such a theory of derivation, precisely where they stand without it. . . . Mr. Darwin, in proposing a theory which suggests a *how* that harmonizes these facts into a system, we trust implies that all was done wisely, in the largest sense designedly, and by an Intelligent First Cause. The contemplation of the subject on the intellectual side, the

---

*[Editor's note: Gray's third difficulty was a complicated objection concerning the sterility of crosses between species.]

amplest exposition of the Unity of Plan in Creation, considered irrespective of natural agencies, leads to no other conclusion.

We are thus, at last, brought to the question; what would happen if the derivation of species were to be substantiated, either as a true physical theory, or as a sufficient hypothesis? What would come of it? The enquiry is a pertinent one, just now. For, of those who agree with us in thinking that Darwin has not established his theory of derivation, many will admit with us that he has rendered a theory of derivation much less improbable than before; that such a theory chimes in with the established doctrines of physical science, and is not unlikely to be largely accepted long before it can be proved. Moreover, the various notions that prevail,—equally among the most and the least religious,—as to the relations between natural agencies or phenomena and Efficient Cause, are seemingly more crude, obscure, and discordant than they need be.

It is not surprising that the doctrine of the book should be denounced as atheistical. What does surprise and concern us is, that it should be so denounced by a scientific man,* on the broad assumption that a material connection between the members of a series of organized beings is inconsistent with the idea of their being intellectually connected with one another through the Deity, i.e., as products of one mind, as indicating and realizing a preconceived plan. An assumption the rebound of which is somewhat fearful to contemplate, but fortunately one which every natural birth protests against.

It would be more correct to say, that the theory in itself is perfectly compatible with an atheistic view of the universe. That is true; but it is equally true of physical theories generally. Indeed, it is more true of the theory of gravitation, and of the nebular hypothesis, than of the hypothesis in question. The latter merely takes up *a particular, proximate cause*, or set of such causes, from which, it is argued, the present diversity of species has or may have *contingently* resulted. The author does not say *necessarily* resulted; that the actual results in mode and measure, and none other must have taken place. On the other hand the theory of gravitation, and its extension in the nebular hypothesis, assume a *universal and ultimate* physical cause, from which the effects in nature must *necessarily* have resulted. Now it is not thought, at least at the present day, that the establishment of the Newtonian theory was a step towards

---

*[Editor's note: Gray was here referring to Agassiz.]

atheism or pantheism. Yet the great achievement of Newton consisted in proving that certain forces, (blind forces, so far as the theory is concerned,) acting upon matter in certain directions, must *necessarily* produce planetary orbits of the exact measure and form in which observation shows them to exist;—a view which is just as consistent with eternal necessity, either in the atheistic or the pantheistic form, as it is with theism.

Nor is the theory of derivation particularly exposed to the charge of the atheism of fortuity; since it undertakes to assign real causes for harmonious and systematic results. But of this, a word at the close.

The value of such objections to the theory of derivation may be tested by one or two analogous cases. The common scientific as well as popular belief is that of the original, independent creation of oxygen and hydrogen, iron, gold, and the like. Is the speculative opinion, now increasingly held, that some or all of the supposed elementary bodies are derivative or compound, developed from some preceding forms of matter, irreligious? Were the old alchemists atheists as well as dreamers in their attempts to transmute earth into gold? Or, to take an instance from force (power),—which stands one step nearer to efficient cause than form—was the attempt to prove that heat, light, electricity, magnetism, and even mechanical power are variations or transmutations of one force, atheistical in its tendency? The supposed establishment of this view is reckoned as one of the greatest scientific triumphs of this century. . . .

In our opinion, then, it is far easier to vindicate a theistic character for the derivative theory, than to establish the theory itself upon adequate scientific evidence. Perhaps scarcely any philosophical objection can be urged against the former to which the nebular hypothesis is not equally exposed. Yet the nebular hypothesis finds general scientific acceptance, and is adopted as the basis of an extended and recondite illustration in Mr. Agassiz's great work.

How the author of this book harmonizes his scientific theory with his philosophy and theory, he has not informed us. Paley,* in his celebrated analogy with the watch, insists that if the time-piece were so constructed as to produce other similar watches, and after the manner of generation in animals, the argument from design

---

*[Editor's note: William Paley (1743–1805) was an English philosopher whose *View of the Evidences of Christianity* (1794) was the most elaborate presentation of the argument for design. Paley compared the world to a watch, and argued that the discovery of such a mechanism compelled men to believe in an intelligent watchmaker.]

would be all the stronger. What is to hinder Mr. Darwin from giving Paley's argument a further *a-fortiori* extension to the supposed case of a watch which sometimes produces better watches, and contrivances adapted to successive conditions, and so at length turns out a chronometer, a town-clock, or a series of organisms of the same type? From certain incidental expressions at the close of the volume, taken in connection with the motto adopted from Whewell,* we judge it probable that our author regards the whole system of nature as one which had received at its first formation the impress of the will of its Author, foreseeing the varied yet necessary laws of its action throughout the whole of its existence, ordaining when and how each particular of the stupendous plan should be realized in effect, and—with Him to whom to will is to do—in ordaining doing it. Whether profoundly philosophical or not, a view maintained by eminent philosophical physicists and theologians ... will hardly be denounced as atheism.

We wished under the light of such views, to examine more critically the doctrine of this book, especially of some questionable parts;—for instance, its explanation of the natural development of organs, and its implication of a "necessary acquirement of mental power" in the ascending scale of gradation. But there is room only for the general declaration that we cannot think the Cosmos a series which began with chaos and ends with mind, or of which mind is a result: that if by the successive origination of species and organs through natural agencies, the author means a series of events which succeed each other irrespective of a continued directing intelligence, —events which mind does not order and shape to destined ends, —then he has not established that doctrine, nor advanced towards its establishment, but has accumulated improbabilities beyond all belief. Take the formation and the origination of the successive degrees of complexity of eyes as a specimen. The treatment of this subject upon one interpretation is open to all the objections referred to; but if, on the other hand, we may rightly compare the eye "to a telescope, perfected by the long continued efforts of the highest human intellects," we could carry out the analogy, and draw satisfactory illustrations and inferences from it. The essential, the directly

---

*[Editor's note: William Whewell (1794–1866) was an English logician and philosopher of science, from whom Darwin took an epigram for the *Origin*: "But with regard to the material world, we can at least go so far as this—we can perceive that events are brought about not by insulated interpositions of Divine power, exertated in each particular case, but by the establishment of general laws."]

intellectual thing is the making of the improvements in the telescope or the steam-engine. Whether the successive improvements, being small at each step, and consistent with the general type of the instrument, are applied to some of the individual machines, or entire new machines are constructed for each, is a minor matter. Though if machines could engender, the adaptive method would be most economical; and economy is said to be a paramount law in nature. The origination of the improvements, and the successive adaptations to meet new conditions or subserve other ends, are what answer to the supernatural, and therefore remain inexplicable. As to bringing them into use, though wisdom foresees the result, the circumstances and the natural competition will take care of that, in the long run. The old ones will go out of use fast enough, except where an old and simple machine remains still best adapted to a particular purpose or condition. . . . If there's a Divinity that shapes these ends, the whole is intelligible and reasonable; otherwise, not.

The work is a scientific one, rigidly restricted to its direct object; and by its science it must stand or fall. Its aim is, probably, not to deny creative intervention in nature,—for the admission of the independent origination of certain types does away with all antecedent improbability of as much intervention as may be required, —but to maintain that Natural Selection in explaining the facts, explains also many classes of facts which thousandfold repeated independent acts of creation do not explain, but leave more mysterious than ever. How far the author has succeeded, the scientific world will in due time be able to pronounce.

CHAPTER 2

The Religious Issue

Dogmatic – UNWARRANTED STUBBORNESS OF OPINION.

INTRODUCTION

When professional scientists like Agassiz and Gray debated evolution, their arguments were colored by an obvious and pained concern over the religious implications of Darwinism. When other kinds of people who were only incidentally interested in science entered the debate, they quickly made the religious issue their central focus. For those American intellectuals who had serious religious commitments—institutional or intellectual, and often both—the stakes were supremely high. The *Origin*, more than any scientific book before or since, seemed to Darwin's contemporaries to have the most profound sorts of consequences for faith. To some, these consequences appeared disastrous. To others, Darwinism pointed a hopeful way toward radical and sometimes bizarre reformulations of theology.

Whichever way people leaned, they did not, in the 1870s and 1880s, quarrel at great length over the question of the origin of man (which Darwin did not discuss in the *Origin*) or over the reality of the human soul (which Darwin and most of his followers never denied). The religious debate centered, instead, on the concept of design, on the question of whether any sort of supernatural intelligence ruled over or within creation, giving it purpose and meaning. The *Origin* could easily be interpreted as a description of nature as what Darwin called a "tangled bank," with no purposes higher than a brute struggle for survival. Confronting this potent horror, theologians and religiously minded philosophers had three options. First, they could simply deny the truth of the theory of evolution, on scientific or dogmatic grounds. Second, they could attempt to harmonize religion and biology by arguing that Darwin had just described in better detail than Scripture the operations of God in the world. Or, finally, they could insist that biology and religion had nothing to do with one another, that religious truth

31

was "spiritual" and scientific truth "material," and that there could be neither harmony nor conflict between them. A great majority of working clergymen and religious laymen took the first option and simply refused to believe in evolution even if they understood it. But among clergymen who could lay any claim at all to being intellectuals, among theologians in the better seminaries and divinity schools, and among philosophers with a religious turn of mind, the acceptance of Darwinism kept fairly close pace with its acceptance as orthodoxy among scientists.

Those religious leaders who did reject Darwinism were most often men who, like Agassiz, had made their careers before 1859 and so already had invested their careers and reputations in a pre-Darwinian view of life. Charles Hodge (1797–1878), author of one of the most insistent religious attacks on evolution, was sixty-two years old when the *Origin* was published. In his book *What Is Darwinism?* (1874), he returned a straightforward answer to the question of his title: "It is atheism." But by the time Hodge published this verdict, he was already part of a shrinking minority of theologians. His career and his world view were both rigid and confined. He spent most of his life at Princeton, from 1811 to his death in 1878, first as a student and then as a professor in the Theological Seminary. His ways of thinking were as severely constricted as the geography of his career. His most famous boast [PRAISE ONESE] was that no new idea had ever originated in the Princeton Theological Seminary. And his own students, like Agassiz's, drifted away from his position to surrender to the Darwinian revolution in science. By 1885, one of the best known clergymen in America, Henry Ward Beecher, could declare blandly that "the period of controversy is passed and closed." For the intellectual leaders of American religion, the question by the 1880s was not whether to accept Darwinism but what implications to draw from it, whether to try to incorporate evolutionary theory into religious doctrine, or to declare religion altogether independent of science.

The most obvious way to salvage something of orthodoxy was to take the path of independence, to accept evolution as a valid scientific theory but to interpret Scripture and dogma in such a way that *no* findings of science could ever weaken faith. This solution— which had been gathering strength since the age of Copernicus, Galileo, and Newton—amounted to a narrowing of the claims of religion over knowledge in order to preserve the "inner" and "spiritual" truths of Christianity. In the twentieth century, this sort of intellectual compartmentalization has become so habitual in American denominations and churches that it is almost an intellectual reflex. But in the 1870s and 1880s, despite centuries of preparation for the step, it was still a radical and professionally risky maneuver. James Woodrow (1828–1907), who was the uncle of President Woodrow Wilson, was Professor of Natural Science in Connection with Divinity at the Presbyterian Seminary of Columbia, South Carolina. In 1884, he was asked by the seminary's governing board to declare himself on the question of evolution. He chose to make his reply in an address to the seminary's alumni association. Woodrow had studied biology under Agassiz, but he was thoroughly convinced by the *Origin*. He tried, in his talk, to give himself and his former students a way out of the Darwinian trap. By simply recognizing two wholly different kinds of truth, scientific and spiritual, he argued, they could coolly accept the findings of science and still keep their faith intact.

In the short run, Woodrow's gamble failed. His speech resulted in the loss of his professorship and set off a feud between pro- and anti-Darwinian Presbyterian ministers in the South. Woodrow had to prove his orthodoxy in a series of religious trials. In the end, he not only maintained his standing as a minister but became head of the governing body of the Presbyterian churches of South Carolina. He also managed to save a reputation for soundness in the centers of secular power, and seven years after his controversial address he was appointed president of the University of South Carolina. The atmosphere that bred the anti-evolution laws of the 1920s and brought about the Scopes "monkey" trial in Dayton, Tennessee, was not yet a problem for Woodrow and men like him in the 1880s. The reason was simple: most lay people had not even heard enough about Darwinism to feel threatened by it, so state legislators were under no significant pressure to protect Biblical conceptions of creation in the schools.

Woodrow was a generation younger than Hodge, but for all their difference in age both men encountered the *Origin* after they had matured and established themselves in a career. For younger people, reading the *Origin* and the other literature of evolution was part of growing up. For college students in the 1860s and early 1870s, becoming a partisan of Darwin, or of his disciples and popularizers, was a titillating excursion into intellectually dangerous waters. In the middle third of the nineteenth century, most men in the United States still entered college with the ministry in mind as a possible career. Most of the college presidents and many of the professors held degrees in divinity, and in such an atmosphere, a

titillating – excite pleasurably.

RACY - RISQUÉ -

clever lad could, by becoming a Darwinian, acquire a small but racy reputation as an infidel. In the end, however, most young men were still unwilling to go so far as to repudiate religion altogether. As they matured, if they became professional academics or writers, their usual course was to discover and teach some sort of harmony between evolution and what they thought of as the essential and permanent spiritual core of religion. The result of this search for harmony was the development of an often strange new theology, in which all the anthropomorphic and transcendental qualities of God were sacrificed to science, but in which the evolutionary process on a cosmic scale was itself transformed into an object of worship and a source for morality. It became possible and even fashionable to speak of God as a "World-spirit" or a "Biologos," gradually coming into being in a universe where evolution was law at all levels from the microscopic to the celestial.

Most of the men who devised these evolutionary theologies took their intellectual cues not primarily from Darwin but from the English philosopher Herbert Spencer. Spencer's conceptual stock-in-trade was what he called a "synthetic philosophy." It attempted to absorb Darwinian evolution into a universal process of development, in which everything from stars to human societies participated. According to Spencer, the universe and everything in it was gradually developing from a simple and homogeneous state into a complex and articulated state. The articulated or heterogeneous solar system, for example, had developed from a nebulous cloud of undifferentiated matter. Highly complex forms of life had emerged from relatively simple and unarticulated one-celled organisms. To preside over this evolving universe, Spencer postulated the existence of an "unknowable" force or energy, acting always and on everything, absolute and eternal. It was simple enough to think of such an absolute force as God, to deify the evolutionary process, and to make it yield, in the end, the same sorts of values that had been inherent to pre-Darwinian Christianity.

The busiest and most popular American promoter of such evolutionary theologies was John Fiske (1842–1901). Fiske practically made a career out of Darwinism. Before he graduated from Harvard in 1863, he was threatened with expulsion because of his aggressive promotion of "infidel" science and philosophy. He trained for the law and passed the Massachusetts bar, but his real career was that of popular lecturer on American history and what he called "the cosmic philosophy"—his reconciliation of evolution, religion, and Christian morality. He delivered the talk on "Herbert

POSTULATED - ASSUMPTION

Spencer's Service to Religion," which appears in this chapter, in 1882. The occasion was a grand banquet in New York for Herbert Spencer, a climactic celebration of his visit to the United States. Scores of leaders of business, journalism, and academic life gathered to pay Spencer tribute. The atmosphere was robust, complacent, well-fed, and self-congratulatory. The diners and speakers were men who might have suffered mildly in the past for their acceptance of Darwinism, but who now were plainly in control of affairs and opinions. Among such men, and among many other readers of Spencer's *Synthetic Philosophy*, no doubt was left that Darwinism and Spencer's extensions of it had been successfully domesticated and absorbed into a world view fit for men who were genteel, Victorian, and, loosely speaking, Christian. When Henry Ward Beecher ended the banquet with a promise to meet Herbert Spencer beyond the grave, he struck a note perfectly suited to the attitudes and expectations of the diners, who greeted the remark with smiling and hearty applause. Spencer, in his turn, luxuriated in the fact that his amiable and reassuring version of evolution had become so respectable. When Fiske finished his talk on the philosopher's service to faith, Spencer rose from his chair and voiced warm approval of the way Fiske resolved the conflict of science and religion.

A Catholic variant of Fiske's position was worked out by Father John Zahm (1851–1921), in an effort to reconcile evolution and Church dogma. Zahm, who was one of America's most energetic churchmen and scholars, developed his argument most fully in *Evolution and Dogma* (1896), which is excerpted in this chapter. Zahm's sense of the problem was somewhat like Woodrow's: that is, he argued that religion need never to fear the findings of science because science and Scripture could never really conflict. But Zahm went further, to a position very like Fiske's, to argue that evolution actually supported dogma by requiring man to presuppose the existence of an intelligent and purposeful God. Zahm also tried to accomplish a third task, which neither Fiske nor Woodrow had to take up: he attempted to show that evolution was not only consistent with dogma, but also was the best interpretation which could be put in the writings and sayings of the Church's great patristic and medieval saints and doctors, men like Gregory of Nyssa, Augustine, Francis of Assisi, and above all, Thomas Aquinas. The *Origin* was already an old book when Zahm published *Evolution and Dogma*, and he adopted a very conciliatory tone toward the Church's conservatives. But even though his book gained a quick and considerable audience in Europe, it still was placed on the *Index* of rejected writings by theological authorities in Rome.

The three intellectual opinions exercised by Hodge, Woodrow, Fiske, and Zahm were enough to satisfy almost everyone. There was, however, a fourth choice possible for people who had no interest in keeping religious coals warm. Some intellectuals—usually young and aggressive men—seized on the theory of evolution as just one more piece of evidence of the incompatibility of religion and science. Such a man was Lester Frank Ward (1841–1913) who became, in the 1880s and the 1890s, one of the most notable social philosophers in the United States. But in 1870–1871, he was a brash young government clerk just completing a night-school education. He was also a leader of the National Liberal Reform League, a secret society of skeptical men who desired "the mental emancipation of mankind from the trammels of superstition." The League published a self-consciously avant-garde newsletter, *The Iconoclast*, with Ward as its editor and chief contributor. The tone of *The Iconoclast* was earnest and brittle, and its principal mission during its short year-and-a-half life was to turn primarily Spencerian weapons on religious orthodoxy. Ward, in the three little essays that are included in this chapter, and in his other efforts for *The Iconoclast*, did not attempt to prove that scientific findings contradicted specific religious doctrines. He argued, instead, that the general spirit of scientific inquiry was opposed to the traditional attitudes of religion, and that the opposition was an irreconcilable difference of intellectual styles. This did not mean, however, that Ward was prepared to give up every sentimental ideal in favor of a clinically ruthless critique of men's values and dreams. He was easily able to discover sanctions within science for notions like "progress," "brotherhood," and the other nonsupernatural ethical ingredients of the Christianity of his day. His program, in effect, was to abandon the idea of God in order to promote the possibility of a scientific morality.

Iconoclast – Attacker of cherished beliefs; or institutions.

WHAT IS DARWINISM?*

Charles Hodge

This is a question which needs an answer. Great confusion and diversity of opinion prevail as to the real views of the man whose writings have agitated the whole world, scientific and religious. If a man says he is a Darwinian, many understand him to avow himself virtually an atheist; while another understands him as saying that he adopts some harmless form of the doctrine of evolution. This is a great evil.

It is obviously useless to discuss any theory until we are agreed as to what that theory is. The question, therefore, What is Darwinism? must take precedence of all discussion of its merits.

The great fact of experience is that the universe exists. The great problem which has ever pressed upon the human mind is to account for its existence. What was its origin? To what causes are the changes we witness around us to be referred? As we are a part of the universe, these questions concern ourselves. What are the origin, nature, and destiny of man? . . . Mr. Darwin undertakes to answer these questions. He proposes a solution of the problem which thus deeply concerns every living man. Darwinism is, therefore, a theory of the universe, at least so far as the living organisms on this earth are concerned. . . .

The Scriptural solution of the problem of the universe is stated in words equally simple and sublime: "In the beginning God created the heavens and the earth." We have here, first, the idea of God. The word God has in the Bible a definite meaning. It does not stand for an abstraction, for mere force, for law or ordered sequence. God is a spirit, and as we are spirits, we know from consciousness that God is, (1.) A Substance; (2.) That He is a person; and, therefore, a self-conscious, intelligent, voluntary agent. He can say I; we can address Him as Thou; we can speak of Him as He or Him. This idea of God pervades the Scriptures. It lies at the foundation of natural religion. It is involved in our religious consciousness. It enters essentially into our sense of moral obligation. It is inscribed ineffaceably, in letters more or less legible, on the heart of every human being. The man who is trying to be an atheist is trying to free himself from the laws of his being. He might as well try to free himself from liability to hunger or thirst.

The God of the Bible, then, is a Spirit, infinite, eternal, and

---

*(New York: Scribner, Armstrong and Company, 1874), *passim*.

unchangeable in his being, wisdom, power, holiness, goodness, and truth. As every theory must begin with some postulate, this is the grand postulate with which the Bible begins. This is the first point.

The second point concerns the origin of the universe. It is not eternal either as to matter or form. It is not independent of God. It is not an evolution of his being, or his existence form. He is extramundane as well as antemundane. The universe owes its existence to his will.

Thirdly, as to the nature of the universe; it is not a mere phenomenon. It is an entity, having real objective existence, or actuality. This implies that matter is a substance endowed with certain properties, in virtue of which it is capable of acting and of being acted upon. These properties being uniform and constant, are physical laws to which, as their proximate causes, all the phenomena of nature are to be referred.

Fourthly, although God is extramundane, He is nevertheless everywhere present. That presence is not only a presence of essence, but also of knowledge and power. He upholds all things. He controls all physical causes, working through them, with them, and without them, as He sees fit. As we, in our limited spheres, can use physical causes to accomplish our purposes, so God everywhere and always cooperates with them to accomplish his infinitely wise and merciful designs.

Fifthly, man as part of the universe, is, according to the Scriptures, as concerns his body, of the earth. So far, he belongs to the animal kingdom. As to his soul, he is a child of God, who is declared to be the Father of the spirit of all men. God is a spirit, and we are spirits. We are, therefore, of the same nature with God. We are God-like; so that in knowing ourselves we know God. No man conscious of his manhood can be ignorant of his relationship to God as his Father.

The truth of this theory of the universe rests, in the first place, so far as it has been correctly stated, on the infallible authority of the Word of God. In the second place, it is a satisfactory solution of the problem to be solved: (1.) It accounts for the origin of the universe. (2.) It accounts for all the universe contains, and gives a satisfactory explanation of the marvellous contrivances which abound in living organisms, of the adaptations of these organisms to conditions external to themselves, and for those provisions for the future, which on any other assumption are utterly inexplicable. (3.) It is in conflict with no truth of reason and with no fact of experience. (4.) The Scriptural doctrine accounts for the spiritual nature of man, and meets all his spiritual necessities. It gives him an object of adoration, love, and confidence. It reveals the Being on whom his indestructible sense of responsibility terminates. The truth of this doctrine, therefore, rests not only on the authority of the Scriptures, but on the very constitution of our nature. The Bible has little charity for those who reject it. It pronounces them to be either derationalized or demoralized, or both. . . .

We have not forgotten Mr. Darwin. It seemed desirable, in order to understand his theory, to see its relation to other theories of the universe and its phenomena, with which it is more or less connected. His work on the "Origin of Species" does not purport to be philosophical. . . . Darwin does not speculate on the origin of the universe, on the nature of matter, or of force. He is simply a naturalist, a careful and laborious observer; skillful in his descriptions, and singularly candid in dealing with the difficulties in the way of his peculiar doctrine. He set before himself a single problem, namely, How are the fauna and flora of our earth to be accounted for? In the solution of this problem, he assumes:

1. The existence of matter, although he says little on the subject. Its existence however, as a real entity, is everywhere taken for granted.

2. He assumes the efficiency of physical causes, showing no disposition to resolve them into mind-force, or into the efficiency of the First Cause.

3. He assumes also the existence of life in the form of one or more primordial germs. He does not adopt the theory of spontaneous generation. What life is he does not attempt to explain. . . .

4. To account for the existence of matter and life, Mr. Darwin admits a Creator. This is done explicitly and repeatedly. Nothing, however, is said of the nature of the Creator and of his relation to the world, further than is implied in the meaning of the word.

5. From the primordial germ or germs (Mr. Darwin seems to have settled down to the assumption of only one primordial germ), all living organisms, vegetable and animal, including man, on our globe, through all the stages of its history, have descended.

6. As growth, organization, and reproduction are the functions of physical life, as soon as the primordial germ began to live, it began to grow, to fashion organs, however simple, for its nourishment and increase, and for the reproduction, in some way, of living forms like itself. How all living things on earth, including the endless variety of plants, and all the diversity of animals—insects, fishes, birds, the ichthyosaurus, the mastodon, the mammoth, and man—have descended from the primordial animalcule, he thinks, may be accounted for by the operation of the following natural laws:

First, the law of Heredity, or that by which like begets like. The offspring are like the parent.

Second, the law of Variation, that is, while the offspring are, in all essential characteristics, like their immediate progenitor, they nevertheless vary more or less within narrow limits, from their parent and from each other. Some of these variations are indifferent, some deteriorations, some improvements, that is, they are such as enable the plant or animal to exercise its functions to greater advantage.

Third, the law of Over Production. All plants and animals tend to increase in a geometrical ratio; and therefore tend to overrun enormously the means of support. . . . Hence of necessity arises a struggle for life. Only a few of the myriads born can possibly live.

Fourth, here comes in the law of Natural Selection, or the Survival of the Fittest. That is, if any individual of a given species of plant or animal happens to have a slight deviation from the normal type, favorable to its success in the struggle for life, it will survive. This variation, by the law of heredity, will be transmitted to its offspring, and by them again to theirs. Soon these favored ones gain the ascendency, and the less favored perish; and the modification becomes established in the species. After a time another and another of such favorable variations occur, with like results. Thus very gradually, great changes of structure are introduced, and not only species, but genera, families, and orders in the vegetable and animal world, are produced. Mr. Darwin says he can set no limit to the changes of structure, habits, instincts, and intelligence, which these simple laws in the course of millions or milliards of centuries may bring into existence. He says, "we cannot comprehend what the figures 60,000,000 really imply, and during this, or perhaps a longer roll of years, the land and waters have everywhere teemed with living creatures, all exposed to the struggle for life, and undergoing change." . . . Years in this connection have no meaning. We might as well try to give the distance of the fixed stars in inches. As astronomers are obliged to take the diameter of the earth's orbit as the unit of space, so Darwinians are obliged to take a geological cycle as their unit of duration. . . .

We have not yet reached the heart of Mr. Darwin's theory. The main idea of his system lies in the word "natural." He uses that word in two senses: first, as antithetical to the word artificial. Men can produce very marked varieties as to structure and habits of animals. This is exemplified in the production of the different breeds of horses, cattle, sheep, and dogs; and specially, as Mr. Darwin seems to think, in the case of pigeons. . . . If, then, he argues, man, in a comparatively short time, has by artificial selection produced all these varieties, what might be accomplished on the boundless scale of nature, during the measureless ages of the geologic periods?

Secondly, he uses the word natural as antithetical to supernatural. Natural selection is a selection made by natural laws, working without intention and design. It is, therefore, opposed not only to artificial selection, which is made by the wisdom and skill of man to accomplish a given purpose, but also to supernatural selection, which means either a selection originally intended by a power higher than nature; or which is carried out by such power. In using the expression Natural Selection, Mr. Darwin intends to exclude design, or final causes. All the changes in structure, instinct, or intelligence, in the plants or animals, including man, descended from the primordial germ, or animalcule, have been brought about by unintelligent physical causes. On this point he leaves us in no doubt. . . . It is affirmed that natural selection is the operation of natural laws, analogous to the action of gravitation and of chemical affinities. It is denied that it is a process originally designed, or guided by intelligence, such as the activity which foresees an end and consciously selects and controls the means of its accomplishment. Artificial selection, then, is an intelligent process; natural selection is not.

There are in the animal and vegetable worlds innumerable instances of at least apparent contrivance, which have excited the admiration of men in all ages. There are three ways of accounting for them. The first is the Scriptural doctrine, namely, that God is a Spirit, a personal, self-conscious, intelligent agent; that He is infinite, eternal, and unchangeable in his being and perfections; that He is ever present; that this presence is a presence of knowledge and power. In the external world there is always and everywhere indisputable evidence of the activity of two kinds of force: the one physical, the other mental. The physical belongs to matter, and is due to the properties with which it has been endowed; the other is the everywhere present and ever acting mind of God. To the latter are to be referred all the manifestations of design in nature, and the ordering of events in Providence. This doctrine does not ignore the efficiency of second causes; it simply asserts that God overrules and controls them. Thus the Psalmist says, "I am fearfully and wonderfully made. . . . My substance was not hid from thee, when I was made in secret, and curiously wrought . . . in the lower parts of the earth. Thine eyes did see my substance yet being imperfect; and in thy book all my members were written, which in continuance were fashioned, when as yet there were none of them." . . . He sends rain, frost, and snow. He controls the winds and the waves. He determines the casting of the lot, the flight of an arrow, and the falling of a sparrow. This universal and constant control of God is not only one of the most patent and pervading doctrines of the Bible, but it is one of the fundamental principles of even natural religion.

The second method of accounting for contrivances in nature admits that they were foreseen and purposed by God, and that He endowed matter with forces which He foresaw and intended should produce such results. But here his agency stops. He never interferes to guide the operation of physical causes. He does nothing to control the course of nature, or the events of history. . . . Paley indeed says, that if the construction of a watch be an undeniable evidence of design it would be a still more wonderful manifestation of skill, if a watch could be made to produce other watches; and, it may be added, not only other watches, but all kinds of time-pieces in endless variety. So it has been asked, if man can make a telescope, why cannot God make a telescope which produces others like itself? This is simply asking, whether matter can be made to do the work of mind? The idea involves a contradiction. For a telescope to make a telescope, supposes it to select copper and zinc in due proportions and fuse them into brass; to fashion that brass into inter-entering tubes; to collect and combine the requisite materials for the different kinds of glass needed; to melt them, grind, fashion, and polish them; adjust their densities and focal distances, etc., etc. A man who can believe that brass can do all this, might as well believe in God. . . .

This banishing God from the world is simply intolerable, and, blessed be his name, impossible. An absent God who does nothing is, to us, no God. Christ brings God constantly near to us. . . . It may be said that Christ did not teach science. True, but He taught truth; and science, so called, when it comes in conflict with truth, is what man is when he comes in conflict with God.

The advocates of these extreme opinions protest against being considered irreligious. Herbert Spencer says, that his doctrine of an inscrutable, unintelligent, unknown force, as the cause of all things, is a much more religious doctrine than that of a personal, intelligent, and voluntary Being of infinite power and goodness. Matthew

Arnold* holds that an unconscious "power which makes for right," is a higher idea of God than the Jehovah of the Bible. Christ says, God is a Spirit. . . .

The third method of accounting for the contrivances manifested in the organs of plants and animals, is that which refers them to the blind operation of natural causes. They are not due to the continued cooperation and control of the divine mind, nor to the original purpose of God in the constitution of the universe. This is the doctrine of the Materialists, and to this doctrine, we are sorry to say, Mr. Darwin, although himself a theist, has given in his adhesion. It is on this account the Materialists almost deify him.

From what has been said, it appears that Darwinism includes three distinct elements. First evolution, or the assumption that all organic forms, vegetable and animal, have been evolved or developed from one, or a few, primordial living germs; second, that this evolution has been effected by natural selection, or the survival of the fittest; and third, and by far the most important and only distinctive element of his theory, that this natural selection is without design, being conducted by unintelligent physical causes. . . .

It is however neither evolution nor natural selection, which give Darwinism its peculiar character and importance. It is that Darwin rejects all teleology, or the doctrine of final causes. He denies design in any of the organisms in the vegetable or animal world. He teaches that the eye was formed without any purpose of producing an organ of vision. . . . It is the distinctive doctrine of Mr. Darwin, that species owe their origin, not to the original intention of the divine mind; not to special acts of creation calling new forms into existence at certain epochs; not to the constant and everywhere operative efficiency of God, guiding physical causes in the production of intended effects; but to the gradual accumulation of unintended variations of structure and instinct, securing some advantage to their subjects. . . .

All the innumerable varieties of plants, all the countless forms of animals, with all their instincts and faculties, all the varieties of men with their intellectual endowments, and their moral and religious nature, have, according to Darwin, been evolved by the agency of the blind, unconscious laws of nature. . . . The grand and

---

*[Editor's note: Matthew Arnold (1822–1888) was an English schoolman, poet, and critic who was one of a small handful of writers exercising a compelling sway over the Victorian audience, both British and American.]

fatal objection to Darwinism is this exclusion of design in the origin of species, or the production of living organisms. . . .

The conclusion of the whole matter is, that the denial of design in nature is virtually the denial of God. Mr. Darwin's theory does deny all design in nature, therefore, his theory is virtually atheistical; his theory, not he himself. He believes in a Creator. But when that Creator, millions on millions of ages ago, did something,—called matter and a living germ into existence,—and then abandoned the universe to itself to be controlled by chance and necessity, without any purpose on his part as to the result, or any intervention or guidance, then He is virtually consigned, so far as we are concerned, to nonexistence. . . . This is the vital point. The denial of final causes is the formative idea of Darwin's theory, and therefore no teleologist can be a Darwinian. . . .

We have thus arrived at the answer to our question, What is Darwinism? It is Atheism.

EVOLUTION*

James Woodrow

At the same time that you honored me with an invitation to deliver an address before you on this occasion, the Board of Directors at the Theological Seminary, in view of the fact that "Scepticism in the world is using alleged discoveries in science to impugn the word of God," requested me "to give fully my views, as taught in this institution, upon Evolution, as it respects the world, the lower animals and man." Inasmuch as several members of the Board are also members of this Association, and both Board and Association feel the same interest in the Seminary, I have supposed that I could not select a subject more likely to meet with your approval than the one suggested to me by the Directors. . . . As is intimated in the Board's request, I may assume that your chief interest in the topic is not in its scientific aspects, but in relations it may bear to the word of God; and therefore I will speak mainly of these relations. . . .

---

*From Joseph L. Blau, ed., *American Philosophic Addresses, 1700–1900* (New York: Columbia University Press, 1946), pp. 488–513.

Before entering on the discussion of the specific subject of Evolution in itself and in its relations to the Sacred Scriptures, it may be well to consider the relations subsisting between the teachings of the Scriptures and the teachings of natural science generally. We hear much of the harmony of science and Scripture, of their reconciliation, and the like. Now, is it antecedently probable that there is room for either agreement or disagreement? We do not speak of the harmony of mathematics and chemistry, or of zoology and astronomy, or the reconciliation of physics and metaphysics. Why? Because the subject matter of each of these branches of knowledge is so different from the rest. It is true we may say that some assertion made by astronomy cannot be correct, because it contradicts some known truth of mathematics or of physics. But yet, in such a case, we would not proceed to look for harmony or reconciliation; we would confine ourselves to the task of removing the contradiction by seeking the error which caused it, and which it proved to exist; for we know that, as truth is one, two contradictions cannot both be true.

May it not be that we have here a representation of the probable relations between the Bible and science—that their contents are so entirely different that it is vain and misleading to be searching for harmonies; and that we should confine our efforts to the examination of real or seeming contradictions which may emerge, and rest satisfied, without attempting to go farther, when we have discovered that there is no contradiction, if it was only seeming, or have pointed out the error that caused it, if real?

Let us test this point by examining special cases which have arisen, and with regard to which conclusions satisfactory to all believers in the Bible have now been reached.

In Genesis i. 16, the Bible speaks of the two great lights, the sun and the moon, and of the stars as if these were of comparatively insignificant size and importance. It says further, Joshua x. 13, that "the sun stood still, and the moon stayed"; "the sun stood still in the midst of the heaven, and hasted not to go down about a whole day." In these and other passages the Bible has been thought to teach that the sun and the moon are larger than any of the stars, and that sun, moon, and stars, having been created for the benefit of man, revolve around the earth as a centre. On the scientific side, two forms of astronomy have been presented: the Ptolemaic, teaching that the earth is the centre of the universe; the Copernican, teaching that the sun is the centre of our planetary system.* Those who asked for harmony between science and the Bible found wonderful confirmation of the Bible in the Ptolemaic astronomy, and of the Ptolemaic astronomy in the Bible. But gradually it came to be seen and admitted that, whatever might be its teachings on other subjects, the Bible was at least not intended to teach astronomy; and for centuries general assent has been given to the words of Calvin: "Moses does not speak with philosophical acuteness on occult mysteries, but relates those things which are everywhere observed, even by the uncultivated. . . . He who would learn astronomy, and other recondite arts, let him go elsewhere." . . . The Bible does not teach science; and to take its language in a scientific sense is grossly to pervert its meaning.

As in the example above given, so in all other cases of supposed contradiction of the Bible by science, I have found that the fair honest application of such principles has caused the contradiction to disappear. I have found nothing in my study of the Holy Bible and of natural science that shakes my firm belief in the divine inspiration of every word of that Bible, and in the consequent absolute truth, the absolute inerrancy, of every expression which it contains, from beginning to end. While there are not a few things which I confess myself wholly unable to understand, yet I have found nothing which contradicts other known truth. It ought to be observed that this is a very different thing from saying that I have found everything in the Sacred Scriptures to be in harmony with natural science. To teach this result it would be necessary to know the exact meaning of every part of the Scriptures, and the exact amount of truth in each scientific proposition. But to show that in any case there is no contradiction, all that is needed is to show that a reasonable supposition of what the passage in question may mean does not contradict the proved truth in science. . . .

After these preliminary observations, I proceed to discuss the main subject of this address.

Before answering the question, What do you think of Evolution? I must ask, What do you mean by Evolution?

When thinking of the origin of anything, we may inquire, Did

---

*[Editor's note: Ptolemy was an Egyptian astronomer of the second century A.D., whose model of the universe had the earth stationary at the center, with the moon, sun, planets, and stars moving around it. Nicolaus Copernicus (1473–1543), in a famous tract, *De revolutionibus orbium coelestium* (1543), gave the first recognizably modern account of a sun-centered planetary system.]

it come into existence just as it is? or did it pass through a series of changes from a previous state in order to reach its present condition? For example, if we think of a tree, we can conceive of it as having come immediately into existence just as we see it; or, we may conceive of it as having begun its existence as a minute cell in connexion with a similar tree, and as having reached its present condition by passing through a series of changes, continually approaching and at length reaching the form before us. Or thinking of the earth, we can conceive of it as having come into existence with its present complex character; or we may conceive of it as having begun to exist in the simplest possible state, and as having reached its present condition by passing through a long series of stages, each derived from its predecessor. To the second of these modes, we apply the term "Evolution." It is evidently equivalent to "derivation"; or, in the case of organic beings, to "descent."

This definition or description of Evolution does not include any reference to the power by which the origination is effected; it refers to the mode, and to the mode alone. So far as the definition is concerned, the immediate existence might be attributed to God or to chance; the derived existence to inherent uncreated law, or to an almighty personal Creator, acting according to laws of his own framing. It is important to consider this distinction carefully, for it is wholly inconsistent with much that is said and believed by both advocates and opponents of Evolution. It is not unusual to represent Creation and Evolution as mutually exclusive, as contradictory: Creation meaning the immediate calling out of non-existence by divine power; Evolution, derivation from previous forms or states by inherent, self-originated or eternal laws, independent of all connexion with divine personal power. Hence, if this is correct, those who believe in Creation are theists; those who believe in Evolution are atheists. But there is no propriety in thus mingling in the definition two things which are so completely different. . . .

The definition now given, which seems to me the only one which can be given within the limits of natural science, necessarily excludes the possibility of the questions whether the doctrine is theistic or atheistic, whether it is religious or irreligious, moral or immoral. It would be as plainly absurd to ask these questions as to inquire whether the doctrine is white or black, square or round, light or heavy. In this respect it is like every other hypothesis or theory in science. These are qualities which do not belong to such subjects. The only question that can rationally be put is, Is the doctrine true or false? If this statement is correct—and it is almost if not quite self-evident—it should at once end all disputes not only between Evolution and religion, but between natural science and religion universally. To prove that the universe, the earth, and the organic beings upon the earth, had once been in a different condition from the present, and had gradually reached the state which we now see, could not disprove or tend to disprove the existence of God or the possession by him of a single attribute ever thought to belong to him. How can our belief in this doctrine tend to weaken or destroy our belief that he is infinite, that he is eternal, that he is unchangeable, in his being, or his wisdom, or his power, or his holiness, or his justice, or his goodness, or his truth? Or how can our rejection of the doctrine either strengthen or weaken our belief in him? Or how can either our acceptance or rejection of Evolution affect our love to God, or our recognition of our obligation to obey and serve him—carefully to keep all his commandments and ordinances?

True, when we go outside the sphere of natural science, and inquire whence this universe, questions involving theism forthwith arise. Whether it came into existence immediately or mediately is not material; but what or who brought it into existence? Did it spring from the fortuitous concurrence of eternally-existing atoms? Are the matter and the forces which act upon it in certain definite ways eternal; and is the universe, as we behold it, the result of their blind unconscious operation? Or, on the other hand, was the universe in all its orderly complexity brought into existence by the will of an eternal personal spiritual God, one who is omniscient, omnipresent, omnipotent? These questions of course involve the very foundations of religion and morality; but they lie wholly outside of natural science; and are, I repeat, not in the least affected by the decision of that other question, Did the universe come into its present condition immediately or mediately; instantly, in a moment, or gradually, through a long series of intermediate stages? They are not affected by, nor do they affect, the truth or falsehood of Evolution.

But, admitting that the truth of Theism is not involved in the question before us, it may fairly be asked, Does not the doctrine of Evolution contradict the teachings of the Bible? This renders it necessary to inquire whether the Bible teaches anything whatever as to the mode in which the world and its inhabitants were brought into their present state; and if so, what that teaching is.

It does not seem to be antecedently probable that there would be any specific teaching there on the subject. We have learned that "the Scriptures principally teach what man is to believe concerning God, and what duty God requires of man"; and that "the whole counsel of God, concerning all things necessary for his own glory, man's salvation, faith, and life, is either expressly set down in Scripture, or by good and necessary consequence may be deducted from Scripture." But this does not include the principles of natural science in any of its branches. We have already seen that it certainly does not include the teaching of astronomy or geography; it does not include anatomy or physiology, zoology or botany—a scientific statement of the structure, growth, and classification of animals and plants. Is it any more likely that it includes an account of the limits of the variation which the kinds of plants and animals may undergo, or the circumstances and conditions by which such variation may be affected? We would indeed expect to find God's relation to the world and all its inhabitants set forth; but he is equally the Creator and Preserver, however it may have pleased him, through his creating and preserving power, to have brought the universe into its present state. He is as really and truly your Creator, though you are the descendant of hundreds of ancestors, as he was of the first particle of matter which he called into being, or the first plant or animal, or the first angel in heaven.

So much at least seems clear—that whatever the Bible may say touching the mode of creation, is merely incidental to its main design, and must be interpreted accordingly. Well may we repeat with Calvin, "He who would learn astronomy and other recondite arts, let him go elsewhere."

It is further to be observed, that whatever may be taught is contained in the first part of the oldest book in the world, in a dead language, with a very limited literature; that the record is extremely brief, compressing an account of the most stupendous events into the smallest compass. Now the more remote from the present is any event recorded in human language, the more completely any language deserves to be called dead, the more limited its contemporaneous literature, the briefer the record itself, the more obscure must that record be—the more difficult it must be to ascertain its exact meaning, and especially that part of its meaning which is merely incidental to its main design. . . .

The actual examination of the sacred record seems to me to show that the obscurity exists which might have been reasonably anticipated. It is clear that God is there represented as doing whatever is done. But whether in this record the limitless universe to the remotest star or nebula is spoken of, or only some portion of it, and if the latter, what portion, I cannot tell. And if there is an account of the methods according to which God proceeded in his creative work, I cannot perceive it. It is said *that* God created; but, so far as I can see, it is not said *how* he created. We are told nothing that contradicts the supposition, for example, that, in creating our earth and the solar system of which it forms a part, he brought the whole into existence very much in the condition in which we now see the several parts; or, on the other hand, that he proceeded by the steps indicated in what is called the nebular hypothesis. Just as the contrary beliefs of Calvin and ourselves touching the centre of the solar system fail to contradict a single word in the Bible, so the contrary beliefs of those who accept and those who reject the nebular hypothesis fail to contradict a single word of the Bible.

I regard the same statements as true when made respecting the origin of the almost numberless species of organic beings which now exist and which have existed in the past. In the Bible I find nothing that contradicts the belief that God immediately brought into existence each form independently; or that contradicts the contrary belief that, having originated one or a few forms, he caused all the others to spring from these in accordance with the laws which he ordained and makes operative. . . .

When we reach the account of the origin of man, we find it more detailed. In the first narrative there is nothing that suggests the mode of creating any more than in the case of the earth, or the plants and animals. But in the second, we are told that "the Lord God formed man of the dust of the ground, and breathed into his nostrils the breath of life; and man became a living soul." Here seems to be a definite statement utterly inconsistent with the belief that man, either in body or soul, is the descendant of other organised beings. At first sight the statement, that "man was formed of the dust of the ground," seems to point out with unmistakeable clearness the exact nature of the material of which man's body was made. But further examination does not strengthen this view. For remembering the principles and facts already stated, and seeking to ascertain the meaning of "dust of the ground" by examining how the same words are employed elsewhere in the narrative, the sharp definiteness which seemed at first to be so plainly visible somewhat disappears. For example, we are told in one place that the waters were commanded to bring forth the moving creature that hath life, and fowl that may fly above the earth; and the command was obeyed. And yet, in another place we are told that out of the ground the Lord God formed every beast of the field, and every fowl of the air. Now as both these statements are true, it is evident that there can be no intention to describe the material employed. There was some sort of connexion with the water, and some with the ground; but beyond this nothing is clear. Then further, in the sentence which God pronounced upon Adam, he says: "Out of the ground wast thou taken; for dust thou art, and unto dust shalt thou return." And in the curse uttered against the serpent, it was said: "Dust shalt thou eat all the days of thy life." Now Adam, to whom God was speaking, was flesh and blood and bone; and the food of serpents then as now consisted of the same substances, flesh and blood. The only proper conclusion in view of these facts seems to be that the narrative does not intend to distinguish in accordance with chemical notions different kinds of matter, specifying here inorganic in different states, and there organic, but merely to refer in a general incidental way to previously existing matter, without intending or attempting to describe its exact nature. . . .

As regards the soul of man, which bears God's image, and which differs so entirely not merely in degree but in kind from anything in the animals, I believe that it was immediately created, that we are here so taught; and I have not found in science any reason to believe otherwise. Just as there is no scientific basis for the belief that the doctrine of derivation or descent can bridge over the chasms which separate the non-existent from the existent, and the inorganic from the organic, so there is no such basis for the belief that this doctrine can bridge over the chasm which separates the mere animal from the exalted being which is made after the image of God. The mineral differs from the animal in kind, not merely in degree; so the animal differs from man in kind; and while science has traced numberless transitions from degree to degree, it has utterly failed to find any indications of transition from kind to kind in this sense. . . .

Believing, as I do, that the Scriptures are almost certainly silent on the subject, I find it hard to see how any one can hesitate to prefer the hypothesis of mediate creation to the hypothesis of immediate creation. . . .

I cannot take time to discuss at length objections which have been urged against this hypothesis, but may say that they do not seem to me of great weight. It is sometimes said that, if applied to man, it degrades him to regard him as in any respect the descendant of the beast. We have not been consulted on the subject, and possibly our desire for noble origin may not be able to control the matter; but, however that may be, it is hard to see how dirt is nobler than the highest organisation which God had up to that time created on the earth. And further, however it may have been with Adam, we are perfectly certain that each one of us has passed through a state lower than that of the fish, then successively through states not unlike those of the tadpole, the reptile, and the quadruped. Hence, whatever nobility may have been conferred on Adam by being made of dust has been lost to us by our passing through these low animal stages.

It has been objected that it removes God to such a distance from us that it tends to atheism. But the doctrine of descent certainly applies to the succession of men from Adam up to the present. Are we any farther from God than were the earlier generations of the antediluvians? Have we fewer proofs of his existence and power than they had? It must be plain that, if mankind shall continue to exist on the earth so long, millions of years hence the proofs of God's almighty creative power will be as clear as they are to-day.

It has been also objected that this doctrine excludes the idea of design in nature. But if the development of an oak from an acorn in accordance with laws which God has ordained and executes, does not exclude the idea of design, I utterly fail to see how the development of our complex world, teeming with co-adaptations of the most striking character, can possibly exclude that idea.

I have now presented briefly, but as fully as possible in an address of this kind, my views as to the method which should be adopted in considering the relations between the Scriptures and natural science, showing that all that should be expected is that it shall be made to appear by interpretations which may be true that they do not contradict each other; that the contents and aims of the Scriptures and of natural science are so different that it is unreasonable to look for agreement or harmony; that terms are not and ought not to be used in the Bible in a scientific sense, and that they are used perfectly truthfully when they convey the sense intended; that on these principles all alleged contradictions of natural science by the Bible disappear; that a proper definition of Evolution excludes all reference to the origin of the forces and laws by which it works, and therefore that it does not and cannot affect belief in God or in religion; that, according to not unreasonable interpretations of the Bible, it does not contradict anything there taught so far as regards the earth, the lower animals, and probably man as to his body; that there are many good grounds for believing that Evolution is true in these respects; and lastly, that the reasons urged against it are of little or no weight.

I would say in conclusion, that while the doctrine of Evolution in itself, as before stated, is not and cannot be either Christian or anti-Christian, religious or irreligious, theistic or atheistic, yet viewing the history of our earth and its inhabitants, and of the whole universe, as it is unfolded by its help, and then going outside of it and recognising that it is God's PLAN OF CREATION, instead of being tempted to put away thoughts of him, as I contemplate this wondrous series of events, caused and controlled by the power and wisdom of the Lord God Almighty, I am led with profounder reverence and admiration to give glory and honor to him that sits on the throne, who liveth for ever and ever; and with fuller heart and a truer appreciation of what it is to create, to join in saying, Thou art worthy, O Lord, to receive glory and honor and power; for thou hast created all things, and for thy pleasure they are and were created.

HERBERT SPENCER'S SERVICE TO RELIGION*

John Fiske

We have met here this evening to do homage to a dear and noble teacher and friend, and it is well that we should choose this time to recall the various aspects of the immortal work by which he has earned the gratitude of a world. The work which Herbert Spencer has done in organizing the different departments of human knowledge, so as to present the widest generalizations of all the sciences in a new and wonderful light, as flowing out of still deeper and wider truths concerning the universe as a whole; the great number of profound generalizations which he has established incidentally to the pursuit of this main object; the endlessly rich and suggestive thoughts which he has thrown out in such profusion by the wayside all along the course of this great philosophical enterprise—all this work is so manifest that none can fail to recognize it. It is work of the caliber of that which Aristotle and Newton did; though coming in this latter age, it as far surpasses their work in its vastness of performance as the railway surpasses the sedan chair, or as the

*From Fiske, *Essays, Historical and Literary* (2 vols.; New York: Macmillan, 1902), Vol. II, pp. 227–37.

telegraph surpasses the carrier-pigeon. But it is not of this side of our teacher's work that I wish to speak, but of a side of it that has, hitherto, met with less general recognition.

There are some people who seem to think that it is not enough that Mr. Spencer should have made all these priceless contributions to human knowledge, but actually complain of him for not giving us a complete and exhaustive system of theology into the bargain. What I wish, therefore, to point out is that Mr. Spencer's work on the side of religion will be seen to be no less important than his work on the side of science, when once its religious implications shall have been fully and consistently unfolded. If we look at all the systems or forms of religion of which we have any knowledge, we shall find that they differ in many superficial features. They differ in many of the transcendental doctrines which they respectively preach, and in many of the rules of conduct which they respectively lay down for men's guidance. They assert different things about the universe, and they enjoin or prohibit different kinds of behaviour on the part of their followers. The doctrine of the Trinity, which to most Christians is the most sacred of mysteries, is to all Mohammedans the foulest of blasphemies; the Brahman's conscience would be more troubled if he were to kill a cow by accident, than if he were to swear to a lie or steal a purse; the Turk, who sees no wrong in bigamy, would shrink from the sin of eating pork. But, amid all such surface differences, we find throughout all known religions two points of substantial agreement. And these two points of agreement will be admitted by modern civilized men to be of far greater importance than the innumerable differences of detail.

All religions agree in the two following assertions, one of which is of speculative and one of which is of ethical importance. One of them serves to sustain and harmonize our thoughts about the world we live in, and our place in that world; the other serves to uphold us in our efforts to do each what we can to make human life more sweet, more full of goodness and beauty, than we find it. The first of these assertions is the proposition that the things and events of the world do not exist or occur blindly or irrelevantly, but that all, from the beginning to the end of time, and throughout the furthest sweep of illimitable space, are connected together as the orderly manifestations of a divine Power, and that this divine Power is something outside of ourselves, and upon it our own existence from moment to moment depends. The second of these assertions is the proposition that men ought to do certain things, and ought to refrain from doing certain other things; and that the reason why some things are wrong to do and other things are right to do is in some mysterious, but very real, way connected with the existence and nature of this divine Power, which reveals itself in every great and every tiny thing, without which not a star courses in its mighty orbit, and not a sparrow falls to the ground.

Matthew Arnold once summed up these two propositions very well when he defined God as "an eternal Power, not ourselves, that makes for righteousness." This twofold assertion, that there is an eternal Power that is not ourselves, and that this Power makes for righteousness, is to be found, either in a rudimentary or in a highly developed state, in all known religions. In such religions as those of the Esquimaux . . . this assertion is found in a rudimentary shape on each of its two sides,—the speculative side and the ethical side; in such religions as Buddhism or Judaism it is found in a highly developed shape on both its sides. But the main point is that in all religions you find it in some shape or other. I said, a moment ago, that modern civilized men will all acknowledge that this two-sided assertion, in which all religions agree, is of far greater importance than any of the superficial points in which religions differ. It is really of much more concern to us that there is an eternal Power, not ourselves, that makes for righteousness, than that such a Power is onefold or threefold in its metaphysical nature, or that we ought not to play cards on Sunday, or to eat meat on Friday. No one, I believe, will deny so simple and clear a statement as this. But it is not only we modern men, who call ourselves enlightened, that will agree to this. I doubt not even the narrow-minded bigots of days now happily gone by would have been made to agree to it if they could have had some doggedly persistent Socrates to cross-question them. . . . What men in past times have really valued in their religion has been the universal twofold assertion that there is a God, who is pleased with the sight of the just man and is angry with the wicked every day, and when men have fought with one another, and murdered or calumniated one another for heresy about the Trinity or about eating meat on Friday, it has been because they have supposed belief in the nonessential doctrines to be inseparably connected with belief in the essential doctrine. In spite of all this, however, it is true that in the mind of the uncivilized man, the great central truths of religion are so densely overlaid with hundreds of trivial notions respecting dogma and ritual, that his perception of the great central truths is obscure. These great central truths, indeed, need to be clothed in a dress of little rites and superstition, in order to take hold of his dull and untrained intelligence. But in proportion as men become more civilized, and learn to think more accurately, and to take wider views of life, just so do they come to value the essential truths of religion more highly, while they attach less and less importance to superficial details.

Having thus seen what is meant by the essential truths of religion, it is very easy to see what the attitude of the doctrine of evolution is toward these essential truths. It asserts and reiterates them both; and it asserts them not as dogmas handed down to use by priestly tradition, not as mysterious intuitive convictions of which we can render no account to ourselves, but as scientific truths concerning the innermost constitution of the universe—truths that have been disclosed by observation and reflection, like other scientific truths, and that accordingly harmonize naturally and easily with the whole body of our knowledge. The doctrine of evolution asserts, as the widest and deepest truth which the study of nature can disclose to us, that there exists a power to which no limit in time or space is conceivable, and that all the phenomena of the universe, whether they be what we call material or what we call spiritual phenomena, are manifestations of this infinite and eternal Power. Now this assertion, which Mr. Spencer has so elaborately set forth as a scientific truth—nay, as the ultimate truth of science, as the truth upon which the whole structure of human knowledge philosophically rests—this assertion is identical with the assertion of an eternal Power, not ourselves, that forms the speculative basis of all religions. When Carlyle* speaks of the universe as in very truth the star-domed city of God, and reminds us that through every crystal and through every grass blade, but most through every living soul, the glory of a present God still beams, he means pretty much the same thing that Mr. Spencer means, save that he speaks with the language of poetry, with language coloured by emotion, and not with the precise, formal, and colourless language of science. By many critics who forget that names are but the counters rather than the hard money of thought, objections have been raised to the use of such a phrase as the Unknowable, whereby to describe the power that is manifest in every event of the universe. Yet, when the Hebrew prophet declared that "by him were laid the foundations of the deep," but reminded us "Who by searching can find him out?"

---

*[Editor's note: Thomas Carlyle (1795–1881) was a Scots essayist and man of letters, extremely popular in both Great Britain and the United States.]

he meant pretty much what Mr. Spencer means when he speaks of a power that is inscrutable in itself, yet is revealed from moment to moment in every throb of the mighty rhythmic life of the universe.

And this brings me to the last and most important point of all. What says the doctrine of evolution with regard to the ethical side of this twofold assertion that lies at the bottom of all religion? Though we cannot fathom the nature of the inscrutable Power that animates the world, we know, nevertheless, a great many things that it does. Does this eternal Power, then, work for righteousness? Is there a divine sanction for holiness and a divine condemnation for sin? Are the principles of right living really connected with the intimate constitution of the universe? If the answer of science to these questions be affirmative, then the agreement with religion is complete, both on the speculative and on the practical side; and that phantom which has been the abiding terror of timid and superficial minds—that phantom of the hostility between religion and science—is exorcised now and forever. Now, science began to return a decisively affirmative answer to such questions as these when it began, with Mr. Spencer, to explain moral beliefs and moral sentiments as products of evolution. For clearly, when you say of a moral belief or a moral sentiment, that it is a product of evolution, you imply that it is something which the universe through untold ages has been labouring to bring forth, and you ascribe to it a value proportionate to the enormous effort it has cost to produce it. Still more, when with Mr. Spencer we study the principles of right living as part and parcel of the whole doctrine of the development of life upon the earth; when we see that in an ultimate analysis that is right which tends to enhance fulness of life, and that is wrong which tends to detract from fulness of life—we then see that the distinction between right and wrong is rooted in the deepest foundations of the universe; we see that the very same forces, subtle, and exquisite, and profound, which brought upon the scene the primal germs of life and caused them to unfold, which through countless ages of struggle and death have cherished the life that could live more perfectly and destroyed the life that could only live less perfectly, until humanity, with all its hopes, and fears, and aspirations, has come into being as the crown of all this stupendous work—we see that these very same subtle and exquisite forces have wrought into the very fibres of the universe those principles of right living which it is man's highest function to put into practice. The theoretical sanction thus given to right living is incomparably the most powerful that has ever been assigned in any philosophy of ethics.

Human responsibility is made more strict and solemn than ever, when the eternal Power that lives in every event of the universe is thus seen to be in the deepest possible sense the author of the moral law that should guide our lives, and in obedience to which lies our only guarantee of the happiness which is incorruptible—which neither inevitable misfortune nor unmerited obloquy can ever take away. I have but barely touched upon a rich and suggestive topic. When this subject shall once have been expounded and illustrated with due thoroughness—as I earnestly hope it will be within the next few years—then I am sure it will be generally acknowledged that our great teacher's services to religion have been no less signal than his services to science unparalleled as these have been in all the history of the world.

EVOLUTION AND DOGMA*

John Augustine Zahm

Can a Catholic, can a Christian of any denomination, consistently with the faith he holds dear, be an evolutionist; or is there something in the theory that is so antagonistic to faith and Scripture as to render its acceptance tantamount to the denial of the fundamental tenets of religious belief? The question . . . has been answered both affirmatively and negatively. But, as is evident, the response cannot be both yea and nay. It must be one or the other, and the query now is, which answer is to be given, the negative or the affirmative?

Whatever may be the outcome of the controversy, whatever may be the results of future research and discovery, there is absolutely no room for apprehension respecting the claims and authority of Scripture and Catholic Dogma. Science will never be able to contradict aught that God has revealed; for it is not possible that the Divine works and the Divine words should ever be in any relation to each other but one of the most perfect harmony. Doubts and difficulties may obtain for a time; the forces of error may for a while appear triumphant; the testimonies of the Lord may be tried to the uttermost; but in the long run it will always be found, as has so often been the case in the past, that the Bible and faith, like truth,

*(Chicago: D. H. McBride & Co., 1896), pp. xiv–xix, 378–434.

will come forth unharmed and intact from any ordeal, however severe, to which they may be subjected. For error is impotent against truth; the pride of man's intellect is of no avail against the wisdom of the Almighty. . . . The fictions of opinions are ephemeral, but the testimonies of the Lord are everlasting. . . .

I am not unaware of the fact that Evolution has had suspicion directed against it, and odium cast upon it, because of its materialistic implications and its long anti-Christian associations. I know it has been banned and tabooed because it has received the cordial *imprimatur* of the advocates of Agnosticism, and the special commendation of the defenders of Atheism; that it has long been identified with false systems of philosophy, and made to render yeoman service in countless onslaughts against religion and the Church, against morality and free-will, against God and His providential government of the universe. But this does not prove that Evolution is ill-founded or that it is destitute of all elements of truth. Far from it. It is because Evolution contains so large an element of truth, because it explains countless facts and phenomena which are explicable on no other theory, that it has met with such universal favor, and that it has proved such a powerful agency in the dissemination of error and in giving verisimilitude to the most damnable of doctrines. Such being the case, ours is the duty to withdraw the truth from its enforced and unnatural alliance, and to show that there is a sense in which Evolution can be understood—in which it must be understood, if it repose on a rational basis—in which, far from contributing to the propagation of false views of nature and God, it is calculated to render invaluable aid in the cause of both science and religion. From being an agency for the promulgation of Monism, Materialism and Pantheism, it should be converted into a power which makes for righteousness and the exaltation of holy faith and undying truth. . . .

The evolutionary idea is not . . . the late development it is sometimes imagined to be. On the contrary, it is an idea that had its origin in the speculations of the earliest philosophers, and an idea which has been slowly developed by the studies and observations of twenty-five centuries of earnest seekers after truth.

In reading over the history of Greek philosophy, we are often surprised to see how the sages of old Hellas anticipated many of the views which are nowadays so frequently considered as the result of nineteenth century research. . . . No one can read of the achievements of Aristotle, or recall his marvelous anticipations of modern discoveries, without feeling that it was he who supplied the germs of what subsequently became such large and beautiful growths. As one of the greatest, if not the greatest, of the world's intellects, he accomplished . . . far more than is usually attributed to him, especially in all that concerns the now famous theory of Evolution. . . . In the Stagirite's* doctrines, too, we find the germs of those views on creation which were developed later on with such wonderful fullness, and in such marvelous perfection, by those great Doctors of the Church, Gregory of Nyssa, Augustine and Thomas Aquinas. According to Aristotle it was necessary, that is, in compliance with natural law, that germs, and not animals, should have been first produced; and that from these germs all forms of life, from polyps to man, should be evolved by the operation of natural causes. How like St. Augustine's teaching, that God in the beginning created all things potentially . . . and that these were afterwards developed through the action of secondary causes . . . during the course of untold ages. . . .

No; it is a mistake to suppose that the theory of Evolution, whether cosmic or organic, is something new and the product solely of modern research. It is something old, as old as speculative thought, and stripped of all explanations and subsidiary adjuncts, it is now essentially what it was in the days of Aristotle, St. Augustine, and the Angel of the Schools.** Modern research has developed and illustrated the theory, has given it a more definite shape and rendered it more probable, if indeed it has not demonstrated its truth, but the central idea remains practically the same. . . .

Darwinism . . . is not Evolution; neither is Lamarckism nor Neo-Lamarckism. The theories which go by these names, as well as sundry others, are but tentative explanations of the methods by which Evolution has acted, and of the processes which have obtained in the growth and development of the organic world. They may be true or false, although all of them undoubtedly contain at least an element of truth, but whether true or false, the great central conception of Evolution remains unaffected. . . . What shall ultimately be the fate of the arguments now so confidently advanced in favor of Evolution by its friends, and against it by its enemies, only the future can decide. The grounds of defense and attack will, no doubt, witness many and important changes. Future research and discovery will reveal the weakness of arguments that are now

---

*[Editor's note: "The Stagirite" refers to Aristotle.]
**[Editor's note: "The Angel of the Schools" was Aquinas.]

considered unassailable, and expose the fallacies of others which, as at present viewed, are thoroughly logical. But new reasons in favor of Evolution will be forthcoming in proportion as the older ones shall be modified or shown to be untenable. And, as the evolutionary idea shall be more studied and developed, the objections which are now urged against it will, I doubt not, disappear or lose much of their cogency. . . .

In proportion as Evolution shall be placed on a solider foundation, and the objections which are now urged against it shall disappear, so also will it be evinced, that far from being an enemy of religion, it is, on the contrary, its strongest and most natural ally. Even those who have no sympathy with the traditional forms of belief, who are, in principle, if not personally, opposed to the Church and her dogmas, perceive that there is no necessary antagonism between Evolution and faith, between the conclusions of science and the declarations of revelation. Indeed, so avowed an opponent of Church and Dogma as Huxley informs us that: "The doctrine of Evolution does not even come into contact with Theism, considered as a philosophical doctrine. That with which it does collide, and with which it is absolutely inconsistent, is the conception of creation which theological speculators have based upon the history narrated in the opening book of Genesis."

In other words, Evolution is not opposed to revelation, but to certain interpretations of what some have imagined to be revealed truths. It is not opposed to the dogmas of the Church, but to the opinions of certain individual exponents of Dogma, who would have us believe that their views of the Inspired Record are the veritable expressions of Divine truth.

To say that Evolution is agnostic or atheistic in tendency, if not in fact, is to betray a lamentable ignorance of what it actually teaches, and to display a singular incapacity for comprehending the relation of a scientific induction to a philosophical—or, more truthfully, an anti-philosophical—system. . . . Rather should it be affirmed that Evolution, in so far as it is true, makes for religion and Dogma; because it must needs be that a true theory of the origin and development of things must, when properly understood and applied, both strengthen and illustrate the teachings of faith. "When from the dawn of life," says Prof. Fiske, who is an ardent evolutionist, "we see all things working together towards the Evolution of the highest spiritual attributes of man, we know, however the words may stumble in which we try to say it, that God is in the deepest sense a moral being." Elsewhere the same writer truly observes:

"The doctrine of Evolution destroys the conception of the world as a machine. It makes God our constant refuge and support, and nature His true revelation." And again he declares: "Though science must destroy mythology, it can never destroy religion; and to the astronomer of the future, as well as to the Psalmist of old, the heavens will declare the glory of God."

Evolution does, indeed, to employ the words of Carlyle, destroy the conception of "an absentee God, sitting idle, ever since the first Sabbath, at the outside of His universe and seeing it go." But it compels us to recognize that "this fair universe, were it in the meanest province thereof, is, in very deed, the star-domed city of God; that through every star, through every glass-blade, and most, through every living soul, the glory of a present God still beams." . . .

But the derivation of man from the ape, we are told, degrades man. Not at all. It would be truer to say that such derivation ennobles the ape. Sentiment aside, it is quite unimportant to the Christian "whether he is to trace back his pedigree directly or indirectly to the dust." St. Francis of Assisi, as we learn from his life, "called the birds his brothers." Whether he was correct, either theologically or zoologically, he was plainly free from that fear of being mistaken for an ape which haunts so many in these modern times. Perfectly sure that he, himself, was a spiritual being, he thought it at least possible that birds might be spiritual beings, likewise incarnate like himself in mortal flesh; and saw no degradation to the dignity of human nature in claiming kindred lovingly with creatures so beautiful, so wonderful, who, as he fancied, "praised God in the forest, even as angels did in heaven."

Many, it may here be observed, look on the theory of Evolution with suspicion, because they fail to understand its true significance. They seem to think that it is an attempt to account for the origin of things when, in reality, it deals only with their historical development. . . . Evolution, then, postulates creation as an intellectual necessity, for if there had not been a creation there would have been nothing to evolve, and Evolution would, therefore, have been an impossibility. And for the same reason, Evolution postulates and must postulate, a Creator, the sovereign Lord of all things, the Cause of causes. . . . But Evolution postulates still more. . . . To suppose that simple brute matter could, by its own motion or by any power inherent in matter as such, have been the sole efficient cause of the Evolution of organic from inorganic matter, of the higher from the lower forms of life, of the rational from the irrational creature, is to suppose that a thing can give what it does not possess, that the greater is contained in the less, the superior in the inferior, the whole in a part.

No mere mechanical theory, therefore, however ingenious, is competent to explain the simplest fact of development. Not only is such a theory unable to account for the origin of a speck of protoplasm, or the germination of a seed, but it is equally incompetent to assign a reason for the formation of the smallest crystal or the simplest chemical compound. Hence, to be philosophically valid, Evolution must postulate a Creator not only for the material which is evolved, but it must also postulate a Creator . . . for the power or agency which makes any development possible. God, then, not only created matter in the beginning, but He gave it the power of evolving into all forms it has since assumed or ever shall assume.

But this is not all. In order to have an intelligible theory of Evolution, a theory that can meet the exacting demands of a sound philosophy as well as of a true theology, still another postulate is necessary. We must hold not only that there was an actual creation of matter in the beginning, that there was a potential creation which rendered matter capable of Evolution, in accordance with the laws impressed by God on matter, but we must also believe that creative action and influence still persist, that they always have persisted from the dawn of creation, that they, and they alone, have been efficient in all the countless stages of evolutionary progress from atoms to monads, from monads to man.

This ever-present action of the Deity, this immanence of His in the work of His hands, this continuing in existence and developing of the creatures He has made, is what St. Thomas calls the "Divine administration," and what is ordinarily known as Providence. It connotes the active and constant cooperation of the Creator with the creature, and implies that if the multitudinous forms of terrestrial life have been evolved from the potentiality of matter, they have been so evolved because matter was in the first instance proximately disposed for Evolution by God Himself, and has ever remained so disposed. . . . Evolution, therefore, is neither a "philosophy of mud," nor "a gospel of dirt," as it has been denominated. So far, indeed, is this from being the case that, when properly understood, it is found to be a strong and useful ally of Catholic Dogma. For if Evolution be true, the existence of God and an original creation follow as necessary inferences.

SCIENCE VERSUS THEOLOGY*

Lester Ward

Science is the great Iconoclast. Lord Bacon,** the founder of inductive science, commenced the work of purification by breaking up the idols of the human intellect. He found it necessary before his "Great Restoration" could begin to destroy the Idols of the Tribe, the Den, the Market, and the Theater. Ever since his day, science has been continuing the work of image-breaking. Steadily pursuing its course, turning neither to the right nor to the left, it has already revolutionized the world. . . . But its especial tendency—we do not say its aim—is to purify, if not to supersede, the whole system of theology which has so long prevailed over mankind. And though it does not attack theology, still it is to-day shaking its very foundations.

The aim of science, pre-eminently and exclusively, is to know the truth. It has no prejudices; it rides no hobbies; it clings to no pet ideas. It is ready to sacrifice its most cherished theories the moment they are found not to square with that one great standard, truth. It is willing to labor; it is not sluggish, or delicate, or puffed up. It digs its treasures out of the bowels of the earth, or seeks them amid the hazy nebulae of heaven. It toils and delves and asks no praise from man, no favor shown of God. But this is perhaps no more than the stoics did; no more than the pilgrim or the monk has done. But a tree is known by its fruits.

The candid world is beginning to compare the fruits of theology with those of science. And what does it find? It finds that theology, though as old as human history, has brought few if any beneficial results; while on the other hand, its manifold evils lie scattered all along its pathway. Take from its history all the details of its wars, its conquests, its persecutions, and its massacres, and there would be nothing left but the graves of its hundred million

---

*From Ward, *Glimpses of the Cosmos* (3 vols.; New York: G. P. Putnam's Sons, 1913), Vol. II, pp. 53–55, 74–76, 110–12.

**[Editor's note: Francis Bacon, Lord Chancellor of England (1561–1626) wrote a famous brief for experimental ways of thinking, *Novum organum* (1620). In it, he attacked four "idols" which militated against the advance of knowledge: the idols of the tribe, or fallacious ways of thinking which belong to all men by virtue of their human nature; the idols of the cave, or individual habits of error and faulty perception; the idols of the market, or the tyranny of inadequate languages; and the idols of the theater, or received orthodoxies.]

victims, and the magnificent temples and costly tombs which it has taken the bread from the mouths of a starving world for four thousand years to erect.

Turning from such a picture to the result of scientific labor, behold the contrast! Scarce three hundred years have sufficed to transform the whole aspect of society. To enumerate the results of the application of the power of steam and electricity, so apparent to all, and so often alluded to as to have almost become hackneyed, would give but a meager idea indeed of what science has done to elevate, enlighten, and happify mankind. Its magic wand has touched almost every known object in nature—and many but for it unknown —and they have taken forms of beauty, of convenience, and of usefulness. Brilliant gas jets have superseded the dim and unsightly tapers and candles of the past; elegant fuel-saving stoves have supplanted the ancient chimney places; a thousand labor-saving machines relieve the weary limbs of toiling men and women, while countless factories, mills, and machine shops are supplying fabrics of every description to enhance the comfort and increase the enjoyment of mankind.

We can scarcely fix our mind upon one temporal blessing that we enjoy to-day, from the luxury of good food to the luxury of good health, for which we are not indebted to science. But besides these countless physical blessings science affords the highest and purest intellectual delight. It has led us into the arena of the infinite universe, and taught us to contemplate the wonders of nature, from the vast firmament of revolving spheres to the infinitesimal world of moving atoms; from the sparkling crystal to the living organism, the contemplation of which sublime truths yields to the mind a holier ecstasy than any reflections upon the character and attributes of anthropomorphic deities, or any selfish hopes of a future eternity of bliss. And when we remember that which is the crowning glory of science, that with all these blessings she has never cost one human life, one drop of human blood, one pang of human suffering, how long will the world hesitate to pronounce its decision?

•　　•　　•

In the long struggle between scientific truth and theological error the former has steadily been gaining ground. By slow and almost imperceptible degrees the latter has been yielding and drawing in its lines upon its ultimate fastnesses of faith. The time has now come when we may take a retrospective view of the field, and note the chief advantages of the campaign.

The triumph of the Copernican theory of astronomy, as foreshadowed by Copernicus and demonstrated by Galileo, over that of Ptolemy, as taught by that astronomer in Egypt, and clung to with such desperation by the Christian Church, may be regarded the first of great importance. The Ptolemaic theory that the earth was flat and stationary, and that the sun, moon, and stars revolved around it as a center, was peculiarly adapted to support the statements respecting these things made in the Hebrew Bible. The Hebrew writers were none of them either scientific or philosophical. Like everybody else at the time they wrote, they were totally ignorant of all such matters, without the Grecian shrewdness of avoiding allusion to things of which they were so completely in the dark. Hence they often spoke of them, and always just as they appeared to them. In such a state of ignorance, the theory often referred to was the most natural and the first to develop itself. Agreeing as it did with the Bible, it was eminently satisfactory to the Christian world, and they naturally regarded with jealousy any attempt to supersede it by a new or contrary theory. Hence they resisted the Copernican theory that the earth revolves upon its axis and in an orbit, together with all the rest of the present consistent philosophy of the solar system. "What!" said they, "is the earth after all only a little fraction of the universe; is it a mere satellite revolving around the sun, smaller than several of the planets; is the sun, which the Bible tells us was created to rule the day for man's benefit, a vast world, thousands of times greater than the earth, and stationary with respect to it? This cannot be; this must not be. It would be a death blow to the Bible. This heresy must be suppressed."

We all know with what determination they carried out this purpose. The persecution of the authors of this great discovery is a fact in history which is familiar to every school girl, and a stain which can never be wiped out. But the heresy has triumphed; and to-day he would be deemed a fool, whether Christian, Jew, or Infidel, who would still aver that the earth is flat and stationary. Such is the silent power with which the truth marches on over the dead carcass of religious terror.

To geology we must ascribe the second great victory. The Bible relates, in terms too unequivocal to render it worth while to dispute about their meaning, that the earth was created in six days. Geology tells us, in terms equally unequivocal, that it has been millions of ages in forming. It was, therefore, simply a question of veracity between an old book and the rocks, and again, by a sort of tacit compulsion, the world has given in its adhesion to the testimony of nature. True, the Church has hem'd and haw'd, writhed and twisted its interpretations to adapt them to the newfound truth, but she has been compelled to admit that, whatever may be the meaning of the language of Holy Writ, geology is right anyhow.

The same facts which have overthrown the Hebrew cosmogony have also neutralized the chronology which the wise ecclesiastical genealogists have compiled from the sacred writings. As the former had assigned a ridiculous and puerile period for the antiquity of the earth, so the latter had fixed far too narrow a limit for the antiquity of man. This has been reserved for a more recent but equally signal triumph of science. Sir Charles Lyell, one of the most eminent English geologists, has demonstrated the existence of man for a period of at least 30,000 years upon the continent of Europe, and Professor Agassiz declares that he must have inhabited the peninsula of Florida for as many as ten thousand years. Both these authorities are too great and too conservative to be questioned or impugned, and so we may regard it settled that we have long been led astray by our religious authorities, to be guided at last to the truth only by the hand of science. And this is her third great triumph.

•   •   •

The age of speculation has gone by. The age of investigation has begun. The philosophies of the past have at last culminated in a system which, while it still retains the name philosophy, is in truth, science. . . . The rising school of philosophy, as distinguished from practical scientific labor . . . is that which for want of a better name is styled the Positive. . . . Its aims are all utilitarian, and its principles humanitarian. It is neither dogmatic nor visionary, but liberal and exact. Taking nature as its only source of information, and the phenomena of the universe as the materials for its deductions, it seeks in the observation of their uniformities in the present, to trace all things back to their true origin in the past, and calculate their true destiny in the future.

In this two-fold view it passes in review all the systems and institutions of man upon the earth; follows them back to their natural source in his remote history, and predicts with all necessary certainty their ultimate collapse or triumph. Premising a reign of law as absolute and certain over the affairs of men and nations as over the movements of the celestial spheres, the new philosophy grapples as successfully with the questions of human society, law, government, morals, and religion as with those of astronomy, chemistry, or physics. To reform humanity is the grand object of this system. Its expounders realize their power, by this method, of accomplishing this object. . . . They have caught the true inspiration, as their exact inquiries have revealed to them the great and hitherto hidden secret of human progress in the transcendent majesty of knowledge over all other sources for securing this end; and from each and all of the recognized lights of the Positive Philosophy the cry has gone up for more knowledge, better knowledge! . . . Its laborers are Liberals in the widest sense who, in the very act of building a grand structure with knowledge for its corner-stone, are removing in the most effectual manner the rotten timbers of theological error and popular superstition.

CHAPTER 3

Darwinism and Social Ethics

INTRODUCTION

Intellectuals in the United States used some of the concepts and much of the vocabulary of the theory of evolution as a way of talking scientifically about social, political, and ethical questions. The most common way of describing the resulting discourse is "social Darwinism." The implication of the phrase is usually that Americans seized on Darwinism in order to promote a "cult of individualism" meant to serve as a rationale for a system of competitive, laissez-faire capitalism. Late in the century (according to the conventional version of things), a current of dissent from this prevalent "conservative Darwinism" developed—a dissent often given the name "reform Darwinism." But before the dissent gathered any noticeable force, the initial and significant impact of Darwin's theory was to give ideological legitimacy to the new captains of industry and finance, making their wealth seem to be only the natural result of survival of the fittest. The intellectuals who promoted such ideas were only serving as the apologists for an economic system of uncontrolled competition, making biological excuses for class distinctions and extremes of wealth and poverty. So runs the prevailing account of the intellectual history of the decades after the publication of Darwin's *Origin.*

It is true that in the second half of the nineteenth century great numbers of Americans were ideologically committed to the notions of competition, merited success, and deserved failure. But it is not true that this commitment was based on Darwinian premises. No more than a tiny handful of American business leaders or intellectuals were social Darwinists in any sense precise enough to have a useful meaning. Very few businessmen of the 1870s or 1880s even knew enough of Darwin or Spencer to turn biology to the uses of self-justification. Very few intellectuals were at all interested in defending businessmen and their ways. In business *practice*, at some times and in some industries, a sort of "struggle for survival" and "survival of the fittest" may have been the daily rule. But practice is one thing, and the formulation of explicit rationalizations for conduct is quite another. Either on a popular level or among intellectuals, Darwinian ideas never were put to serious and widespread use in defense of competition and the accumulation of great fortunes.

There was nothing in Darwin's theory to make its direct application to social or economic theory inevitable. Not a single one of the American reviewers of the first edition of the *Origin* made any attempt whatever to discover social ideas in the theory. If competitive capitalism required defending, there were plenty of older ideas ready at hand, ideas that were not tainted with the kind of controversy that the theory of evolution often provoked. The ideals of the Protestant ethic, the widely known maxims of Benjamin Franklin and his imitators, the inherited and conventional economic theory of the followers of Adam Smith—these taken together were more than sufficient to make competition and economic success perfectly respectable.

Neither Darwinism nor Herbert Spencer's cosmic and social extensions of it were exactly easy ideas for untrained nineteenth-century minds to grasp, and the simple difficulty of the subject was enough to prevent social Darwinism from becoming a popular ideology. Worse yet, for anyone who might try to promote an evolutionary justification for capitalism, Darwin's theory was very difficult, if not impossible, to reconcile with the Christian moralism that was almost an official American code. Until at least the 1890s, the system of ethics taught in American colleges and universities was explicitly Christian. Every American who went to college was taught that moral values existed absolutely as divine facts. Furthermore, according to this orthodox moral philosophy, men and women could know what was right and what was wrong only because they had a soul, and with it a conscience, or "moral sense." If the universe as a whole was an evolving fact, as Spencer and his followers claimed, then the idea of objectively permanent moral values was impossible to maintain. And if humans, as all Darwinians came to believe, had descended from the beasts, then it would no longer be reasonable to believe that people really had souls, that spark of divinity which gave them a privileged insight into the good, and differentiated them absolutely from other living creatures. Christian ethics placed primary value on self-sacrifice and not on the values of hedonistic pleasure that were the primary engines of at

HEDONISTIC - WAY OF LIFE DEVOTED TO PLEASURE.

least Spencer's ethical theory. An evolutionary ethics, unless it was elaborately hedged about, could only be a relativist ethics fundamentally out of accord with a conventional Christian world view.

In the middle of the nineteenth century, nearly all the colleges and universities in the United States were headed by men who had been trained as ministers and who often had ministerial careers in conjunction with their academic lives. These men were not only administrative officers but professors, and they managed to put their stamp on college life much more completely than any modern university president is able to do. They taught, typically, the required senior course in moral philosophy, universally considered the capstone of undergraduate education. In this course, and in the textbooks they wrote for it, they tried to inculcate into the students an earnestly Christian view of life. They used their strategic positions to conduct a defensive battle against anything that might smack of social Darwinism. They might accept biological evolution, as most of them did by the 1880s, but evolutionary *ethics* was quite another matter, an infidelity to faith that they resisted vigorously and long.

Noah Porter (1811–1892), who became president of Yale in 1871 and thus presided over the encounter between evolution and his university's protestant orthodoxy, was a typical nineteenth-century college president. He accepted most of the biological theory of evolution. He had his students read Spencer. But the general style of his thought was defensively conservative, a little frightened at what he thought of as the growing radicalism of philosophy. Materialism, positivism, "scientism," and empiricism all were jumbled in his mind, and they all pointed toward the same unchristian conclusion: a relativist view of morals in which nothing remained sacred or stable and in which the only final ground for ethics was what was temporarily adaptive, or what gave pleasure and avoided pain. In his *Elements of Moral Science* (1885), part of which is reprinted below, Porter attempted to give a definitive statement to what he thought was the inescapable opposition between Christian morality and ethical Darwinism or Spencerianism. The *Elements* was a college textbook, and it probably embodied the ethical beliefs of a great majority of academicians in the United States during the 1880s: pious, conservative, abstractly committed to the idea of private property, but not at all interested in constructing a Darwinian rationale for economic competition.

Porter's *Elements* was also typical of American's discussions of the issue in its almost total identification of evolutionary ethics with the name of Herbert Spencer. Spencer's idea of cosmic evolution meant to him that society, like any other fact of life, was subject to the laws of development. This meant, in turn, that ethical values and codes were inevitably rooted in the evolutionary process. From his study of evolution, Spencer derived a wholehearted insistence on laissez-faire competition as the only way of bringing human life into harmony with the cosmic process. According to Spencer, any attempt at social planning or reform was bound to have bad consequences. There was no way to abrogate the laws of struggle and survival of the fittest to suit sentimental hopes for equality and social justice. If competition had unpleasant consequences for many in the present, people of good will could find solace in the hope that the industrial system, left to its own uncontrolled devices, would eventually create plenty, harmony, and perfect freedom from both want and the arbitrary control of one person by another.

Spencer did have American disciples. Indeed, no European philosopher of the nineteenth century had a numerically greater following in the United States. But the vogue of Spencer is not an indication of a vogue for social Darwinism, or for a cult of individualism with a biological basis. Spencer was above all a cosmic philosopher, and it was perfectly possible—in fact it was the normal course for American Spencerians—to be preoccupied with Spencer's guesswork about the universe, and to pay little or no attention to his concrete ethical teachings. The few businessmen who went so far as to contribute money to Spencer, and perhaps even read a little of one of the sets of his books they bought for their libraries, could do so because an acquaintance with him or his philosophy served admirably as a badge of ceremonial familiarity with the upper reaches of culture. Spencer attracted many academic men because of his methodological promise rather than because of his social philosophy. More than anyone writing in English in the 1860s and 1870s, Spencer held out the hope of a "science of society" as rigorous and successful as the natural sciences. It was this methodological aspect of his thought and not his laissez-faire individualism that made him seem such a grandly prophetic philosopher to many of the young economists, sociologists, and anthropologists of the period.

Moreover, even Spencer's competitive individualism was ambiguous. Man began, in Spencer's scheme of things, as an "egoist," but in the end toward which all evolution was advancing, "altruism" would achieve a final and complete conquest of behavior. This ideal outcome, which was the theoretical source of values in Spencer's system, cast considerable doubt on the ultimate virtue of self-interest as an economic or social motive. It was quite possible for an intellectual to accept all of Spencer's cosmic promises and methodological procedures and still derive them from a noncompetitive ethic of self-sacrifice, to make evolutionary ethics almost wholly consistent with the traditions of Christian morality as Porter taught it.

This was the path chosen by John Fiske. If there was a genuine American Spencerian it was Fiske. He was tireless in his praise of Spencer and missed no chance to promote the synthetic philosophy. But Fiske never used Spencerian ideas to endorse the successes of business leaders. When Fiske worked out what seemed to him to be the implications of evolution for ethics, the result was an almost maudlin insistence on self-sacrifice and group solidarity, not a justification of the economic survival of the fittest. Fiske worked out this ethical gloss on Darwin and Spencer in the late 1860s, and he was still preaching it at the end of the century in *Through Nature to God*, a part of which appears in this chapter. He had one important original idea in his long and prolific scholarly life: that the family introduced a moral buffer between the individual and the law of struggle. In the family, he believed, humans developed the "tender" and "benevolent" instincts. And as the family evolved into society, the tendency to love one's neighbor evolved with it. Fiske was, in short, able to perform the same sleight-of-hand on evolutionary ethics as on the religious meaning of Darwinism: he made evolution itself yield moral benevolence, not cruel law for a competitive jungle.

The most famous American attempt to reconcile wealth, the struggle for survival, and the ideal of benevolence was an essay on "Wealth" (1885) by the steel and financial magnate Andrew Carnegie (1835–1919). Carnegie was one of the very few American businessmen who had any real knowledge of Darwin or Spencer. And he did publicly justify competition and success with Darwinian slogans. But Carnegie was also interested in promoting the public reputation of businessmen for ample generosity. For him, the Biblical idea of "stewardship" was even more important to talk about publicly than the idea of the survival of the fittest. Carnegie, like Fiske and like Spencer himself, was a utopian who believed (in principle, at least) that eventually the struggle would cease and people would live together in peace and plenty.

In any case, Carnegie is most interesting because he is most exceptional. He was the only major captain of industry in the Gilded Age who was a clear-cut and articulate social Darwinist.

MAGNATES - MAN OF WEALTH OR POWER.

The most famous social Darwinist statement by a businessman is the remark, often attributed to John D. Rockefeller, that the growth and fortune of a large enterprise was "merely the survival of the fittest," very much like the production by ruthless pruning of the American Beauty rose. But this statement was in fact made not by Rockefeller but by his son, and not during the supposed heyday of social Darwinism but after the turn of the century. Chauncey Depew and James J. Hill, both railroad magnates, did claim that the great corporations were examples of the Darwinian laws of struggle and survival, but their assessments were made in 1910 and 1922, not during the Gilded Age proper (and in books that probably were ghost-written anyway). Carnegie was almost alone among business leaders in his social Darwinism—and even his was carefully modified by the ideal of stewardship.

A much more common use of evolutionary notions than Carnegie's defense of wealth was the academic defense of racism. In fact, the only reality behind the notion of social Darwinism lay exactly here, in the use of a biological theory to justify imperialism and racial discrimination as instances of the survival of the fittest. Darwinian racism took two forms (though the two were often blended and confused). One form was based on the idea that all "races"—and no one was sure what a *race* was, exactly—evolve through a definite progression of "stages." But not all races had evolved on the same schedule. So, such arguments ran, some races had already reached an elevated stage, while others have lagged behind. The second form of Darwinian racism supposed that each race has definite and fixed characteristics that belong to it in the same way that physical attributes belong to every living species. The characteristics of a race included dispositions of every sort, intellectual, emotional, social, and even political. On this view, no two races could ever be alike, and no two races would ever evolve through similar stages, or toward the same result. It was equally clear that some races had always been and would always be superior to others.

Either theory, clearly, made it seem appropriate and just for the "higher" races to dominate the "lower." In fact, according to the racism current among white Europeans and Americans, this domination was not a privilege but a duty. It was, in the astonishingly popular phrasing of the English writer Rudyard Kipling, the "white man's burden," a friendly obligation to try to "educate," "lift," and "civilize" backward and barbaric peoples. While they were being educated and civilized, of course, the duty of the backward and barbaric peoples was to behave themselves, maintain their social distance, and keep their place.

Such ideas had a peculiar relevance for Americans, who were about to take their first steps toward becoming an imperialist rival of European powers. The American experience had always involved a great deal of racial and ethnic domination and bigotry. The United States had been created on the territory of Native Americans, expanded to take in millions of people of Spanish and Indian descent, and built with the labor of black people who were still slaves when Darwin's *Origin* was published. Now, in the decades after 1859, a massive emigration from Eastern and Southern Europe was bringing people of different "races" (as they were routinely called)—Jews, Russians, Poles, Italians and Greeks. Worse yet, from the point of view of those who had come to call themselves "native Americans," was the substantial immigration of Asians. The very words many Americans used to describe this immigration said much about their fear and loathing of it. The immigrants may have been, as the plaque on the Statue of Liberty called them, "huddled masses." But they came in "hordes," hordes that were "teeming" and "swarming."

It was clear that the white "Anglo-Saxons" who dominated American life were threatened at home even as they readied themselves for the promise of imperial adventure abroad. And intellectuals, almost all of them white males who could claim that they came from "Anglo-Saxon stock," responded to the threat and the promise by giving scientific justifications for restricting immigration from Europe, for preventing Asian immigration altogether, for "Americanizing" immigrant children by teaching them contempt for their parents' language, dress, and culture, for "educating" blacks for lives of ignorance and labor, and for taking up the white man's burden wherever the opportunity presented itself.

James K. Hosmer (1834–1927) was one of the leading historians of the United States. His specialty (the specialty of most historians of his generation, in fact) was constitutional history. But, like most of his contemporaries, he did not think of constitutions as written documents or court decisions. For Hosmer, a constitution was an expression of the evolutionary characteristics of a race. And, he believed, each race had a definite political disposition, inherited through countless generations. The peculiar racial tendency of the "Anglo-Saxons" was always and everywhere a tendency toward self-government. This tendency had its inception in the original home of the Anglo-Saxons in a corner of Germany,

Polity -   _INCEPTION- BEGGINING._

where their free men (*eeorls*) owned their own land, and lived together in their settlements (*tuns*), meeting in a free assembly (*moot*) to decide political questions in a democratic fashion. It was carried to England, and it survived through the mixing of the "blood" of Angles and Saxons with Danes, the Normans, and other "races." The Anglo-Saxons' unique capacity for self-government had made its way out into the world, to America, to Australia, to Africa, to every place they went with their distinctive capacity to colonize successfully. So when George Washington took his first oath as president, or when Abraham Lincoln gave the Gettysburg Address, they were only speaking the deep, evolutionary wisdom of their racial "folk." The Constitution of the United States was a kind of codification of racial memory. A New England town meeting was the reenactment of a tun moot.

Hosmer came by his opinions naturally enough. He was a descendant of a family that settled in New England in 1635. He grew up in a small town in Massachusetts, and before he became an academic, he was a minister in another New England village. While he was teaching at Washington University in Saint Louis, Hosmer summarized his arguments in 1890 in *A Short History of Anglo-Saxon Freedom: The Polity of the English-Speaking Race, Outlined in its Inception, Development, Diffusion, and Present Condition*, part of which is reprinted here. In truth, neither his work nor that of other proponents of scientific racism owed much to Darwin's *Origin*. It is much more accurate to say that he was appropriating some of the language of evolution than to say that he was influenced by Darwinism. Even his title, with its "development" and "diffusion," was an attempt to give his ideas the color of science without any of its substance. Only one feature of his work was really indebted to the evolutionary way of thinking: he took an expanding population to be a good evolutionary sign, a sign of domination—as when one says that dinosaurs "ruled" the earth. It was with hope and delight that he announced the calculation that by 1990, there would be a billion people of Anglo-Saxon descent scattered throughout the world, uniquely equipped to govern others because of their inherited and instinctual capacity for self-government.

Hosmer was only one of hundreds—perhaps thousands—of scholars in Europe and the United States who engaged in crackpot theorizing about race, and thought they were doing so on "scientific" grounds that they associated one way or another with evolution. Almost as many intellectuals played the same sort of fast and loose mental games with the distinctions between men and women. And, with only rare exceptions, they all came to the same conclusion: women were biologically inferior to men, and in almost exactly the same ways that everyone else was inferior to northern and western Europeans.

Darwin himself had an apparently happy marriage, and was much in favor of higher education for women. But, in *The Descent of Man* (1874), he made it clear that he believed one of the lessons of evolution was that "Man is more powerful in body and mind than woman." He even introduced a new kind of selection, sexual selection, to complement the method of natural selection in ways he hoped would explain the differences between males and females of the same species. The struggle for survival pitted organisms against each other. Reproduction brought them together, at least briefly. And animals choose—or seem to choose—their mates for reasons that do not always have to do with a superior capacity to get food or defend territory. So, Darwin reasoned, what explains things like brilliant plumage among male birds, or complicated mating behavior in many animal species, is that they evolved as the outcomes of sexual choices. In most species, these choices are made by both males and females (perhaps more often by females than males). But among humans, Darwin believed, men had long ago won the exclusive right to choose. And they had chosen their mates not for reasons that had to do with survival value, like intelligence or strength, but instead for such attributes as "beauty." In effect, Darwin believed that men had engaged in a long program of selective breeding of their own women, and were able to do so because it was the males of the species who engaged directly in the struggle for survival, providing food and shelter for their mates. (It would probably be difficult to find a clearer example of the way a great theorist can translate the myths of his own class and culture directly into "science." In most human cultures, women are treated as inferior creatures. But outside the nineteenth-century upper class in Europe and parts of America, the idea that men can choose their women because men produce and women only reproduce would have been patently absurd.)

Darwin's followers, European and American, worked out an astonishing number of variations on the theme of female inferiority. But they were just that, variations on a theme. Some sought to prove that women's brains were smaller than men's, and when they confronted the fact that women's bodies were also smaller, they did not conclude that women had about the same ratio of brain-to-body weight. Instead, they decided that *both* women's smaller *recapitulates – SUMMARIZE.*

brains and their smaller bodies were the marks of inferiority. Others tried to show that the lower halves of women's faces projected further forward than men's (were more "prognathus"), a sign that women were closer on the evolutionary ladder to the apes and to early man. Darwin and a number of Darwinians also argued that males in most species vary more than females, and used this to explain the "fact" that there were both more idiots and more geniuses among human males than among females. According to this idea, men were the innovative and experimental agents of the race, while women tended to cluster conservatively around the human norm, biologically unable to be Aristotles or Shakespeares. Another very popular way of giving evolutionary support to the idea of female inferiority was to deploy one of the more questionable concepts of the period, the idea that "ontogeny recapitulates phylogeny"—that the individual (ontogeny) passes through the same set of evolutionary stages that the species (phylogeny) has traversed.

This idea had its origins in the observable fact that the human foetus starts as a cell and has, at different stages of development, what look like gills, and a rather definite tail. But proponents of the theory lept from these facts of embryology to history and culture, and argued that the human species had "evolved" not only physically but socially. And this meant that each individual would "recapitulate" the stages of social development as well. The mind of the child would be "savage" or "primitive." Adolescence might represent the glory that was Greece or the grandeur that was Rome. Applied to races, the theory of recapitulation explained that the lower races were simply developmental stages that the higher races had already passed through, and that each individual member of the higher race would recapitulate in childhood. At or near birth, a white European child might be "like" an African. (No one ever seemed to ask what the African "recapitulated" as he or she matured; the answer seemed too obvious: the African was always a child.) Applied to women, the theory was that they might be capable of developing as rapidly as males so far as adolescence, but no further. They were biologically condemned (or privileged, depending on the point of view) to a permanent state of intellectual and emotional immaturity.

One of the most active proponents of the theory of recapitulation—and also of the idea that there were "adolescent races"—was Granville Stanley Hall. He was an eminent psychologist. Indeed, he was the principal inventor of the concept of adolescence—an idea that has always smacked as much of social myth as of scientific reality. Like most of his colleagues in American colleges and universities, he had grown up in a New England town, claimed an "Anglo-Saxon" ancestry, and was ready and willing to use evolutionary ideas to show that white males of his social class happened to be the highest "type" that nature had so far been able to produce. But among the many frauds and confidence men who produced the new "science" of sex and sexuality in the second half of the nineteenth century, he was one of the gentler and more intellectually able. He thought adolescence was the point in life at which people reached the highest "spiritual" development. So saying that women remained morally and mentally at this stage hardly seemed to him to demean them. He believed in higher education for women. In fact, he was deeply sentimental about the set of qualities he thought were truly female: their capacity for "caring" and "sharing," their gentle incapacity for the rough and crude forms of struggle that characterized men. And he was quite willing to blame modern men's "effeminacy" for the growing "mannishness" of their women.

In truth, what Hall did was to look for biological ways of explaining the "sugar and spice and everything nice" stereotype of women that was older than *The Origin of Species*. But he fretted much over the emergence of a new class of educated women who allowed the "stimulations" of intellectual work and competition to distort the "normal" development of their loving and maternal instincts. And he was terrified by the fact that the educated women of his New England were having too few children, and believed this amounted to "race suicide," since the less worthy women of other racial types were outbreeding their superiors. In his *Adolescence* (1904), a part of which is reprinted in this chapter, he attempted to place both his idealization of true womanhood and his anxieties about the new woman in the context of a vaguely Darwinian point of view.

The intellectual consensus on both the inferiority of women and the existence of "lower" races was remarkable. In fact, it may be true that never in the history of the western world had so many highly educated men agreed so warmly (and with such a complete lack of evidence) about anything. And it is certainly true that this twin intellectual consensus was many times as confident and uniform among intellectuals than the other form of social Darwinism, the form that argued that biology provided a justification for capitalism. There was only one important intellectual in America who was an unqualified social Darwinist in this classic meaning of the phrase. He was William Graham Sumner (1840–1910), a profes-

METHODOLOGICAL —

sor of social science at Noah Porter's Yale. When Porter in 1879 challenged Sumner's right to teach from Spencer's *Study of Sociology*, Sumner firmly insisted that he could choose his own course texts, and even threatened to resign. He was almost obsessed by the idea of a science of society, and neither Porter's religious scruples nor any other circumstance would turn him aside. In fact, Sumner was a much clearer example of social Darwinism than even Spencer himself, for Sumner denied the utopian ending that capped Spencer's sociology, and taught that human beings could look forward only to unending and increasingly arduous competition between one another and with nature. Sumner's essay on "Sociology," published first in 1881 and partially reprinted below, is a nicely typical example of his style of social thinking. Like most of his writings, it insists not just on its conclusions, but almost as much on the methodological privileges of sociology as a scientific discipline. The essay also neatly illustrates the fact that Sumner's social "laws" were more often the laws of classical economics than of biology, and were only given added sanction through the introduction of biological arguments and phrases.

In the purity and aggressiveness of his social Darwinism, Sumner was a minority almost of one among American intellectuals. In the last two decades of the century, academic social scientists of a new style were replacing the dominant Noah Porters. These new men— and almost all academics were male—shared much of Sumner's impatience with religious dogma and sentimental thinking about social problems. They were about as deeply preoccupied as Sumner with creating a rigorous science of society. But, almost to a man, the new generation repudiated Sumner's laissez-faire position and opted, instead, for social reform and for communalistic interpretations of society. It was Lester Frank Ward, not Sumner, who in the end had the most to say to the new social science. Ward, who soon outgrew his sophomoric attacks on religion, and who eventually left government service for a professorship at Brown University, was a convinced Darwinian. And in the mid-1870s he had had a decidedly Spencerian cast of mind. But his mature social philosophy, as it was expressed in *Dynamic Sociology* (1883) and other influential books, set Ward at almost perfect odds with Spencer and Sumner. The two most important facts about human life, according to Ward, were that it was social and creative. People did not suffer and struggle alone as individuals. The human race was not a passive victim of natural laws. It was an ingenious aggressor against nature, and its most ingenious strategy was to impose civilization on Darwin's "tangled bank" at every possible point. This creative activity was possible, Ward argued, because of the purposeful function of "Mind as a Social Factor," the title of his best essay, which is reprinted below. Mind separated humans from other creatures just as definitely as life separated organisms from dead matter. And mind was, furthermore, cooperative in its operations and cumulative in its effects. This meant that people did not pit themselves alone against their environment, or against other individuals. Every person inherited not only physical characteristics at birth, but also a grand social stock of power and culture. Every individual's fate was shaped by this social inheritance, much more than by purposeless biological facts; all this made it possible, and even necessary, for men to reduce and control competition and to carefully nourish and preserve those who might be biologically "unfit."

Ward's resolution of the Darwinian problem in social ethics was, in a loose sense, pragmatic. He admitted that there was no ultimate justification for the existence of social and ethical rules, and that mind and culture were developmental outcomes with no discernible purpose outside themselves. He placed great emphasis on the fact that men had created culture and made it *work* more or less successfully. Ward had a somewhat thorny personality, and his books were eccentric in manner. But his theory was as moderate as it was pragmatic. By giving an important place to mind and will, he avoided the determinism that made Spencer and some other naturalistic philosophers of the period so difficult to accept. But Ward did not go to the other extreme, so unattractive to many of the first post-Darwinian generation, to assert the existence of an ideal mind or spirit as a counter-reality to nature. Man, in his scheme of things, could be a part of nature without being the passive victim of its laws or forces. On the other hand, he was able to avoid the increasingly obsolete position that man had a supernatural soul that set him off from the rest of creation.

Ward's separation of nature and culture was very similar to the position taken in one of the most famous lectures on Darwinism ever delivered, Thomas Henry Huxley's "Evolution and Ethics" (1893). Huxley was Darwin's greatest supporter in England, but in "Evolution and Ethics" he attempted to draw a limit to the intellectual impact of the evolutionary theory. There were, Huxley argued (in words that quickly became commonplace among intellectuals in the United States), two distinct processes in which the human species had always participated, the "cosmical" and the "ethical." Evolution, with all its implications of inequality and struggle, belonged

METAPHYSICAL — STUDY OF THE CAUSES AND NATURE OF THINGS.

to the cosmical process. But in society, people set themselves *against* nature. Society, Huxley's "ethical process," was mankind's attempt to break the laws of nature, to establish an artificial clearing in the midst of the mindless jungle of the universe. Nature, then, did not give laws to society, and biology had nothing to teach ethics.

Both Ward and Huxley used the distinction between the natural and the social in such a way as to avoid the choice between scientific determinism and moral freedom. One of the greatest American philosophers, Josiah Royce (1855–1916), responded to Huxley by attempting to force just such a choice. Royce was a neo-Hegelian idealist who taught for most of his life at Harvard, and he was an academic philosopher through and through. He was not much interested, as were Sumner and Ward, in concrete issues of currency, tariff reform, or the uses of government power. Instead, Royce spent most of his years working out formal metaphysical conceptions of the "Absolute." A preoccupation with ivory-tower formalities, however, sometimes breeds a certain abstract kind of intellectual toughness, a refusal to accept sentimental solutions to difficult problems, and a willingness to be intellectually radical. It was this sort of toughness that led Royce to take a position that had no real chance of becoming very influential. He simply denied that science described the real world. The formulas of physics or chemistry, or any other scientific theory served well enough as conventions to help people to go about their business of getting things done. But science—and with it, of course, Darwinism—was *only* a set of conventions. Royce's "real" world was characterized by desire, by chance, and by novelty. His essay "Natural Law, Ethics, and Evolution" (1895), which appears in this chapter, was directed not just at Huxley but at anyone who took science seriously as a point of departure for philosophy. Science, he argued, could proceed only on the assumption of rigorously deterministic regularity in nature. Ethics, to be genuine, had to suppose the existence of contingency, otherwise desire would be only a form of deception, and values would be meaningless illusions. If the cosmical process described by science were real, then the ethical process could only be an irrational figment.

Among them, Fiske, Carnegie, Hosmer, Hall, Sumner, Ward, and Royce almost exhausted the possibilities for assessing the relationship, or lack of one, between Darwinism and social ethics. But there was one alternative left, the most intellectually radical of all, which was seized by the man with the most original mind at work in nineteenth-century America, Charles Sanders Peirce (1839–1914).

CONTINGENCY — POSSIBLE EVENTS.   FIGMENT — SOMETHING IMAGINED OR MADE UP.

Almost everyone who examined the relationship between evolution and ethics asked the same question: what ethical precepts, if any, could be deduced from Darwin's hypothesis? Peirce, with considerable daring, simply reversed the question and asked, what method of evolution would be consistent with man's highest ethical notion, love? Pierce, who was a logician by profession and who has become widely known in the twentieth century as either the founder of pragmatism or as a brilliant forerunner of logical positivism, claimed from the beginning of his career in the 1860s that science was based on logic, but that logic was in turn based on ethics. This meant that man's scientific ways of describing the world were the consequence of prior ethical decisions and leanings. Hence, according to Peirce's extension of this typically pragmatic doctrine, the theory of evolution anyone accepted would depend ultimately on his or her ethical stance. Because the love or "charity" of the New Testament was the most elevated ethical doctrine, Peirce believed interpretations of nature ought to conform to the "gospel" of love—a requirement that Darwin did not meet.

Peirce was born into a well-known Harvard family. His father was a world-famous mathematician, and Peirce spent a number of years on the fringes of the Harvard intellectual community. He also taught briefly at Johns Hopkins University in the early 1880s. But, during much of his life he lived in an almost hermit-like isolation, unable to get or hold an academic position. When he was a young man, Peirce made an intellectual commitment to the ideal of love and to the doctrine that the community is all-important against individual needs and desires. His lonely life was almost a satire on his ethics. As the fact that he was a very much unloved member of no community at all was forced on him, his sense of alienation and his anger at the society from which he was a virtual outcast deepened. By the 1890s, he felt completely out of tune with the America of the Gilded Age, and this sense of alienation came to the surface in an essay on "Evolutionary Love" (1893), a part of which appears in this chapter. In the essay, Peirce abandoned the manner of the cool-headed logician to strike out in resentful prose against the "gospel of greed" that he thought ruled his century and his America.

Darwin's *Origin* probably changed no one's mind about social ethics. Fiske would no doubt have preached self-sacrifice, and Sumner competition, even if the theory of evolution had been delayed by another half-century. Darwinism, like any scientific hypothesis, was wonderfully flexible when men translated it into moral terms, and it could be bent with ease to fit the ethical beliefs that intellectuals had before they read Spencer or Darwin. What distinguished Peirce was that he brought his ethical commitment into the open, and brashly insisted that he would accept no evolutionary theory that did not satisfy the demands of "love" and "community." Darwin's idea of natural selection was "ingenious" and "pretty," Peirce admitted, but it had achieved its dominant position not because of purely scientific merit but merely because it was in harmony with the psychology of greed that controlled the nineteenth-century mind. On this very unscientific ground, Peirce opted away from Darwinism and toward his own peculiar reading of the theory of Jean Baptiste Lamarck.* According to Lamarck, whose *Philosophie Zoologique* preceded the *Origin* by 50 years, the variations that caused changes in species did not occur spontaneously and before birth. Instead, organisms *acquired* variant characters by developing habitual responses to environmental challenges, in the way that a giraffe might acquire a slightly lengthened neck by straining for leaves high on trees. Such acquired variations, Lamarck claimed, could be transmitted by inheritance to the next generation, and, in the long run, could cause species to alter permanently. By 1890, Darwinism had practically driven Lamarck's theory from the field, although late editions of the *Origin* actually incorporated some of Lamarck's ideas. It was an intellectual gamble for Peirce to choose Lamarck over Darwin, but there was one enormous intellectual compensation for the risk. Within Lamarck's theory, Peirce could argue that organisms *purposefully* attempted to acquire useful and beneficial characteristics. Because these efforts benefitted not only the individual organism but the entire species, Lamarckian evolution could be interpreted as evolution by love, in which species behaved like ethical communities, with individual organisms acting not only to serve their own immediate interests, but the long-term interests of their species.

Peirce's emphasis on community and love assumed that both were in principle universal—that not only all people, but all living things, were ethically motivated. It was a view that made little headway.

VARIANT - SOMETHING THAT DIFFERS FROM others of its kind.

*[See Editor's note, p. 18.]

THE ELEMENTS OF MORAL SCIENCE*

Noah Porter

The so-called evolution theory of Ethics is properly classed as one of the theories which derive moral distinctions conspicuously from society by the operation of association, and for the reason that its advocates confessedly make these distinctions to be the products of environment.

Though this environment in its earlier stages is held by them to be material and nervous, yet when it reaches its highest forms it also becomes social. . . . By this formula is explained, in the first place, the emergence . . . of . . . the benevolent or altruistic affection. Its development is thus traced. In the lower forms of existence every impulse would necessarily terminate in the individual self. This must continue to be the case so long as any being is simple in its structure, and so long as it is surrounded by a simple environment with which its communications are rapid and direct. But as the subject becomes more and more complex in structure, and indirect in its communications with its surroundings, it finds that its most important blessings come to it more and more obviously through the medium or influence of other beings than itself. As a consequence, it gradually associates these other beings with all its enjoyments, as sources of blessing to itself, and learns in some sort to regard them as enlargements of its own personal essence, till at a certain time . . . it learns to identify the general well-being with its individual interest. When this process is complete, the common good is inseparably connected with its own highest good. By these successive steps, there emerges a powerful secondary interest in the well-being of others, which at last becomes such a controlling affection as often to take the place of, and dominate over, the primary and individual impulses, and finally to generate . . . pure and disinterested altruism. . . . Heredity also comes in to transmit to succeeding generations the tendencies or powers acquired by the new cerebral stuff which is generated from past human experiences in forms more positive and pure than could possibly be attained by the brains of previous generations. . . .

The objective law or standard of duty is also generated by

---

*From Porter, *The Elements of Moral Science, Theoretical and Practical* (New York: Charles Scribner's Sons, 1885), pp. 118–25, 271–91.

similar processes. . . . So far as it depends on the law of evolution working in and upon the nervous system in which it roots, it is thus explained by Mr. Spencer: "Just in the same way that I believe the intuition of space possessed by any living individual to have arisen from organized and consolidated experiences of all antecedent individuals, who bequeath to him their slowly developed nervous organizations . . . so do I believe that the experiences of utility, organized and consolidated through all past generations of the human race, have been producing corresponding nervous modifications, which, by continued transmission and accumulation, have become in us certain faculties of moral intuition." . . .

It is worthy of notice that this theory also provides for a constant tendency towards what it calls an *absolute morality* under the law of evolution, which shall finally attain to a perfect objective standard and subjective achievement of duty at the end of its progressive march. . . . In other words, the evolutionist's theory of morals presupposes or presumes that the conception of perfect moral excellence as an ideal is the end or aim to which all social arrangements and influences tend and move, even though it be conceded that this has not yet been made real. But how did it come into being as a thought? . . . Especially, how came it to be anticipated . . . in the mind of Mr. Spencer? . . . In other words, if certain ideas concerning the standard of duty and the absolutely perfect virtuous affections, and concerning the law of duty, are known by anticipation as the elements of that absolute morality which is the outcome of completed evolution, how could they have been perfected in the mind of Mr. Spencer, and how came he to be so confident in his belief and knowledge respecting their truth? . . . The very conception of its nature is hidden in the unrevealed future, much more the faith in it as a fact. . . . What it will be, and what it is to be, are problematic ideas and truths, concerning which no man can affirm with positiveness who derives his ethical conceptions from the processes of evolution, whether these processes are wrought in nerve, or mind, or in both. It follows, that any fixed conceptions of moral excellence or moral rules cannot be dependent on the shifting sympathies or associations of our fellow-men, even though these are re-enforced by the activity of brain and nerve, and even though their progress be assumed to be definite and steady towards a goal of absolute moral perfection; or, on the other hand, if there be such a goal, the conception of its nature and the belief in its truths cannot be the growth of the tendencies which it governs and controls, and out of which it is evolved. Neither the idea, nor the belief in it, can precede: both must come after the fact. . . .

It is equally manifest, that the style of virtue which Christianity proposes for man's adoption, and enforces by these motives, is the most thorough-going in its unselfishness, and the most disinterested in its spirit, of any ideal virtue that has ever been conceived by man. . . . Another principle of Christian ethics, which deserves notice, is the doctrine that benevolence, or moral love, comprehends and enforces every duty which man owes to his fellow-man. No single principle is asserted in terms that are at once so philosophical in form and unequivocal in their import as the following: "Owe no man any thing, but to love one another; for he that loveth another hath fulfilled the law." . . . The benevolence taught and exemplified in the Christian ethics is at once the most refined in its emotional quality, and extreme in its disinterestedness. . . .

Not only is the quality of the benevolence which Christianity proposes and prescribes thus refined and idealized, but the energy of its disinterestedness is altogether unique and peculiar. It teaches, in all sobriety and force, "We ought to lay down our lives for the brethren." . . . This extreme of disinterestedness in external action was in its way as novel and peculiar as was the quality of the emotions which animated and impelled it. Under the pagan theory, men could die for their friends, their kindred, and their country, under the motives which the affections for either and all might furnish. But the comprehensive duty of self-sacrifice for our fellow-men was never enforced and recognized as the controlling law of one's active powers, as it is in the Christian system. The family, the friendly, and the patriotic impulses were recognized as noble and as duty-enforcing motives; but their motive power was derived from something short of the relations of human brotherhood, demanding constant self-sacrifice in imitation of that single commanding and moving example to which all Christendom perpetually turns as its symbol and inspiration. . . .

It is sometimes objected, that the Christian ethics are impracticable, because a system so unselfish cannot be applied in a society which is avowedly and actually controlled by principles of self-interest. It is forgotten, that separate and special duties to one's self, to one's family, and country, are entirely consistent, and are even required by the disinterested love of man as man. The objection itself finds all its force in a defective conception of the duties which true benevolence requires. We acknowledge that Christian aims and ideals are higher and purer than those which most men adopt; and that to expect them to do this at once, and thoroughly, would seem romantic if not quixotic. That they are such as very few men exemplify with the energy and consistency which they warrant, is no argument against the practicability of the system itself, but rather an argument for the need of those nobler ideals and that more energetic force which Christianity furnishes, and its disciples respond to. In no other sense can it be true that the Christian ethics are impracticable. Were they adopted at once in the full energy of their fundamental principles, and applied in every possible form to the acts and institutions of humanity, the result in a renovated manhood would demonstrate that they constitute the only practicable ethical system which the world has ever known, or could dream of.

If we compare this system in its theoretic and practical perfection with any and every other which has been painfully wrought out by the ablest and most earnest philosophers—whether with those which were matured in desperate earnestness without the light and inspiration of Christianity, or with those which have been composed in Christendom in ill-disguised but ignorant contempt of its light and wisdom—we cannot but acknowledge its superior insight into the nature of man, and the unmeasured superiority of its speculative profoundness, and its practical adaptations to the various and changing wants and circumstances of humanity. We are also struck with the fact that the best pagan ethics are more allied to the Christian than . . . several well-known modern systems, which, with the New Testament open before their authors, reduce all the phenomena of conscience and duty, all the obligations to law and order, all the restraints upon murder, robbery, and lust, to the relations of mechanism, and the affinities of matter, or the actions and reactions of . . . environment.

THROUGH NATURE TO GOD*

John Fiske

There are few sights in Nature more restful to the soul than a daisied field in June. Whether it be at the dewy hour of sunrise, with blithe matin songs still echoing among the treetops, or while the

---

*(Boston: Houghton Mifflin Co., 1899), pp. 60–130, *passim*.

luxuriant splendour of noontide fills the delicate tints of the early foliage with a pure glory of light, or in that more pensive time when long shadows are thrown eastward and the fresh breath of the sea is felt, or even under the solemn mantle of darkness, when all forms have faded from sight and the night air is musical with the murmurs of innumerable insects, amid all the varying moods through which the daily cycle runs, the abiding sense is of unalloyed happiness, the profound tranquillity of mind and heart that nothing ever brings save the contemplation of perfect beauty. . . .

And yet we need but come a little closer to the facts to find them apparently telling us a very different story. The moment we penetrate below the superficial aspect of things the scene is changed. . . . The life of its countless tiny denizens is one of unceasing toil, of crowding and jostling, where the weaker fall unpitied by the way, of starvation from hunger and cold, of robbery utterly shameless and murder utterly cruel. . . . Of the crawling insects and those that hum through the air, with the quaint snail, the burrowing worm, the bloated toad, scarce one in a hundred but succumbs to the buffets of adverse fortune before it has achieved maturity and left offspring to replace it. The early bird, who went forth in quest of the worm, was lucky if at the close of a day as full of strife and peril as ever knight-errant encountered, he did not himself serve as a meal for some giant foe in the gloaming. When we think of the hawk's talons buried in the breast of the wren, while the relentless beak tears the little wings from the quivering, bleeding body, our mood toward Nature is changed, and we feel like recoiling from a world in which such black injustice, such savage disregard for others, is part of the general scheme. . . .

But as we look further into the matter, our mood is changed once more. We find that this hideous hatred and strife, this whole-sale famine and death, furnish the indispensable conditions for the evolution of higher and higher types of life. . . . The principle of natural selection is in one respect intensely Calvinistic; it elects the one and damns the ninety and nine. In these processes of Nature there is nothing that savours of communistic equality; but "to him that hath shall be given, and from him that hath not shall be taken away even that which he hath." Through this selection of a favoured few, a higher type of life—or at all events a type in which there is more life—is attained in many cases, but not always. Evolution and progress are not synonymous terms. The survival of the fittest is not always a survival of the best or of the most highly organized.

. . . At all events, whenever the type is raised, it is through survival of the fittest, implying destruction to all save the fittest. . . .

The development of civilization, on its political side, has been a stupendous struggle for life, wherein the possession of certain physical and mental attributes has enabled some tribes or nations to prevail over others, and to subject or exterminate them. On its industrial side the struggle has been no less fierce; the evolution of higher efficiency through merciless competition is a matter of common knowledge. Alike in the occupations of war and in those of peace, superior capacity has thriven upon victories in which small heed has been paid to the wishes or the welfare of the vanquished. In human history perhaps no relation has been more persistently repeated than that of the hawk and the wren. The aggression has usually been defended as in the interests of higher civilization, and in the majority of cases the defence has been sustained by the facts. It has indeed very commonly been true that the survival of the strongest is the survival of the fittest.

Such considerations affect our mood toward Nature in a way that is somewhat bewildering. On the one hand, as we recognize in the universal strife and slaughter a stern discipline through which the standard of animate existence is raised and the life of creatures variously enriched, we become to some extent reconciled to the facts. . . . On the other hand, a thought is likely to arise which in days gone by we should have striven to suppress as too impious for utterance; but it is wiser to let such thoughts find full expression, for only thus can we be sure of understanding the kind of problem we are trying to solve. Is not, then, this method of Nature, which achieves progress only through misery and death, an exceedingly brutal and clumsy method? Life, one would think, must be dear to the everlasting Giver of life, yet how cheap it seems to be held in the general scheme of things! In order that some race of moths may attain a certain fantastic contour and marking of their wings, untold thousands of moths are doomed to perish prematurely. Instead of making the desirable object once for all, the method of Nature is to make something else and reject it, and so on through countless ages, till by slow approximations the creative thought is realized. Nature is often called thrifty, yet could anything be more prodigal or more cynical than the waste of individual lives? . . . Upon such a view as this the Cosmic Process appears in a high degree unintelligent, not to say immoral. . . .

Now most assuredly survival of the fittest, as such, has no sort of relation to moral ends. Beauty and ugliness, virtue and vice, are all alike to it. Side by side with the exquisite rose flourishes the hideous tarantula, and in too many cases the villain's chances of livelihood are better than the saint's. . . .

In such a universe we may look in vain for any sanction for morality, any justification for love and self-sacrifice; we find no hope in it, no consolation; there is not even dignity in it, nothing whatever but resistless all-producing and all-consuming energy.

Such a universe, however, is not the one in which we live. In the cosmic process of evolution, whereof our individual lives are part and parcel, there are other agencies at work besides natural selection, and the story of the struggle for existence is far from being the whole story. . . . I think it can be shown that the principles of morality have their roots in the deepest foundations of the universe, that the cosmic process is ethical in the profoundest sense, that in that far-off morning of the world, when the stars sang together and the sons of God shouted for joy, the beauty of self-sacrifice and disinterested love formed the chief burden of the mighty theme. . . .

It must be borne in mind that while the natural selection of physical variations will go far toward explaining the characteristics of all the plants and all the beasts in the world, it remains powerless to account for the existence of man. Natural selection of physical variations might go on for a dozen eternities without any other visible result than new forms of plant and beast in endless and meaningless succession. The physical variations by which man is distinguished from apes are not great. . . . But the moment we consider the minds of man and ape, the gap between the two is immeasurable. . . . How can this overwhelming contrast between psychical and physical difference be accounted for? The clue was furnished by Alfred Russel Wallace,* the illustrious co-discoverer of natural selection. Wallace saw that along with the general development of mammalian intelligence a point must have been reached in the history of one of the primates, when variations of intelligence were more profitable to him than variations in body. . . . Natural selection is the keenest capitalist in the universe; she never loses an instant in seizing the most profitable place for investment, and her judgment is never at fault. Forthwith, for a million years or more

---

*[Editor's note: Alfred Russel Wallace (1823–1913) was a British naturalist who came on the idea of natural selection in 1858, independently of Darwin—who had first sketched out the idea as early as 1842.]

she invested all her capital in the psychical variations of this favoured primate, making little change in his body except so far as to aid in the general result, until by and by something like human intelligence of a low grade, like that of the Australian or the Andaman islander, was achieved. The genesis of humanity was by no means yet completed, but an enormous gulf had been crossed. . . .

But the explanation of the genesis of Humanity is still far from complete. If we compare man with any of the higher mammals, such as dogs and horses and apes, we are struck with several points of difference: *first*, the greater progressiveness of man, the widening of the interval by which one generation may vary from its predecessor; *secondly*, the definite grouping in societies based on more or less permanent family relationships, instead of the indefinite grouping in miscellaneous herds or packs; *thirdly*, the possession of articulate speech; *fourthly*, the enormous increase in the duration of infancy, or the period when parental care is needed. The circumstance last named is the fundamental one, and the others are derivative. It is the prolonged infancy that has caused the progressiveness and the grouping into definite societies, while the development of language was a consequence of the increasing intelligence and sociality thus caused. In the genesis of Humanity the central fact has been the increased duration of infancy. Now, can we assign for that increased duration an adequate cause? I think we can. The increase of intelligence is itself such a cause. A glance at the animal kingdom shows us no such thing as infancy among the lower orders. It is with warmblooded birds and mammals that the phenomena of infancy and the correlative parental care really begin. . . .

We are now prepared to appreciate the marvellous beauty of Nature's work in bringing Man upon the scene. Nowhere is there any breach of continuity in the cosmic process. First we have natural selection at work throughout the organic world, bringing forth millions of species of plant and animal, seizing upon every advantage, physical or mental, that enables any species to survive in the universal struggle. So far as any outward observer, back in the Cretaceous or early Eocene periods, could surmise, this sort of confusion might go on forever. But all at once, perhaps somewhere in the upper Eocene or lower Miocene,* it appears that among the primates, a newly developing family already distinguished for pre-

---

*[Editor's note: Cretaceous, Eocene, and Miocene were geological periods occurring between about 70 million and 160 million years ago.]

hensile capabilities, one genus is beginning to sustain itself more by mental craft and shiftiness than by any physical characteristic. Forthwith does natural selection seize upon any and every advantageous variation in this craft and shiftiness, until this favoured genus of primates, this *Homo Alalus*, or speechless man, as we may call him, becomes preeminent for sagacity, as the mammoth is preeminent for bulk, or the giraffe for length of neck.

In doing this, natural selection has unlocked a door and let in a new set of causal agencies. As Homo Alalus grows in intelligence and variety of experience, his helpless babyhood becomes gradually prolonged, and passes not into sudden maturity, but into a more or less plastic intermediate period of youth. Individual experience, as contrasted with ancestral experience, counts for much more than ever before in shaping his actions, and thus he begins to become progressive. . . . The evidence is abundant that Homo Alalus, like his simian cousins, was a gregarious creature, and it is not difficult to see how, with increasing intelligence, the gestures and grunts used in the horde for signalling must come to be clothed with added associations of meaning, must gradually become generalized as signs of conceptions. This invention of spoken language, the first invention of nascent humanity, remains to this day its most fruitful invention. . . .

With the lengthening of infancy the period of maternal help and watchfulness must have lengthened in correspondence. Natural selection must keep those two things nicely balanced, or the species would soon become extinct. But Homo Alalus had not only a mother, but brethren and sisters; and when the period of infancy became sufficiently long, there were a series of Homunculi Alali, the eldest of whom still needed more or less care while the third and the fourth were arriving upon the scene. In this way the sentiment of maternity became abiding. The cow has strong feelings of maternal affection for periods of a few weeks at a time, but lapses into indifference and probably cannot distinguish her grown-up calves as sustaining any nearer relation to herself than other members of the herd. But Femina Alala, with her vastly enlarged intelligence, is called upon for the exercise of maternal affection until it becomes a permanent part of her nature. In the same group of circumstances begins the permanency of the marital relation. The warrior-hunter grows accustomed to defending the same wife and children and to helping them in securing food. . . .

Thus by gradual stages we have passed from four-footed existence into Human Society. . . . Surely if there is anywhere in the universe a story matchless for its romantic interest, it is the story of the genesis of Man, now that we are at length beginning to be able to decipher it. We see that there is a good deal more in it than mere natural selection. At bottom, indeed, it is all a process of survival of the fittest, but the secondary agencies we have been considering have brought us to a point where our conception of the Struggle for Life must be enlarged. Out of the manifold compounding and recompounding of primordial clans have come the nations of mankind in various degrees of civilization, but already in the clan we find the ethical process at work. The clan has a code of morals well adapted to the conditions amid which it exists. There is an ethical sentiment in the clan; its members have duties toward it; it punishes sundry acts even with death, and rewards or extols sundry other acts. We are, in short, in an ethical atmosphere, crude and stifling, doubtless, as compared with that of a modern Christian homestead, but still unquestionably ethical.

Now, here at last, in encountering the ethical process at work, have we detected a breach of continuity? Has the moral sentiment been flung in from outside, or is it a natural result of the cosmic process we have been sketching? Clearly it is the latter. There has been no breach of continuity. When the prolongation of infancy produced the clan, there naturally arose reciprocal necessities of behaviour among the members of the clan, its mothers and children, its hunters and warriors. If such reciprocal necessities were to be disregarded the clan would dissolve, and dissolution would be general destruction. . . . So for age after age those clans in which the conduct of the individuals is best subordinated to the general welfare are sure to prevail over clans in which the subordination is less perfect. As the maternal instinct had been cultivated for thousands of generations before clanship came into existence, so for many succeeding ages of turbulence the patriotic instinct, which prompts to the defence of home, was cultivated under penalty of death. . . .

Now the moment a man's voluntary actions are determined by conscious or unconscious reference to a standard outside of himself and his selfish motives, he has entered the world of ethics, he has begun to live in a moral atmosphere. Egoism has ceased to be all in all, and altruism—it is an ugly-sounding word, but seems to be the only one available—altruism has begun to assert its claim to sovereignty. In the earlier and purely animal stages of existence it was right enough for each individual to pursue pleasure and avoid pain; it did not endanger the welfare of the species, but on the contrary it favoured that welfare; in its origin avoidance of pain was the surest safeguard for the perpetuation of life, and with due qualifications that is still the case. But as soon as sociality became established, and Nature's supreme end became the maintenance of the clan organization, the standard for the individual's conduct became shifted, permanently and forever shifted. Limits were interposed at which pleasure must be resigned and pain endured, even certain death encountered, for the sake of the clan; perhaps the individual did not always understand it in that way, but at all events it was for the sake of some rule recognized in the clan, some rule which, as his mother and all his kin had from his earliest childhood inculcated upon him, *ought* to be obeyed. This conception of ought, of obligation, of duty, of debt to something outside of self, resulted from the shifting of the standard of conduct outside of the individual's self. Once thus externalized, objectivized, the ethical standard demanded homage from the individual. It furnished the rule for a higher life than one dictated by mere selfishness. . . .

With the evolution of true maternity Nature was ready to proceed to her highest grades of work. Intelligence was next to be lifted to higher levels, and the order of mammals with greatest prehensile capacities, the primates with their incipient hands, were the most favourable subjects in which to carry on this process. The later stages of the marvellous story we have already passed in review. We have seen the accumulating intelligence lengthen the period of infancy, and thus prolong the relations of loving sympathy between mother and child; we have seen the human family and human society thus brought into existence; and along therewith we have recognized the necessity laid upon each individual for conforming his conduct to a standard external to himself. At this point, without encountering any breach of continuity in the cosmic process, we crossed the threshold of the ethical world, and entered a region where civilization, or the gradual perfecting of the spiritual qualities, is henceforth Nature's paramount aim. To penetrate further into this region would be to follow the progress of civilization, while the primitive canoe develops into the Cunard steamship, the hieroglyphic battle-sketch into epics and dramas, sun-catcher myths into the Newtonian astronomy, wandering tribes into mighty nations, the ethics of the clan into the moral law for all men. The story shows us Man becoming more and more clearly the image of God, exercising creative attributes, transforming his physical environment, incarnating his thoughts in visible and tangible shapes all over the world, and extorting from the abysses of space the secrets of vanished ages. From lowly beginnings, without breach of continuity, and through the cumulative action of minute and inconspicuous causes, the resistless momentum of cosmic events has tended toward such kind of consummation; and part and parcel of the whole process, inseparably wrapped up with every other part, has been the evolution of the sentiments which tend to subordinate mere egoism to unselfish and moral ends.

A narrow or partial survey might fail to make clear the solidarity of the cosmic process. But the history of creation, when broadly and patiently considered, brings home to us with fresh emphasis the profound truth of what Emerson once said, that "the lesson of life ... is to believe what the years and the centuries say against the hours; to resist the usurpation of particulars; to penetrate to their catholic sense." When we have learned this lesson, our misgivings vanish, and we breathe a clear atmosphere of faith. Though in many ways God's work is above our comprehension, yet those parts of the world's story that we can decipher well warrant the belief that while in Nature there may be divine irony, there can be no such thing as wanton mockery, for profoundly underlying the surface entanglement of her actions we may discern the omnipresent ethical trend. The moral sentiments, the moral law, devotion to unselfish ends, disinterested love, nobility of soul,—these are Nature's most highly wrought products, latest in coming to maturity; they are the consummation, toward which all earlier prophecy has pointed. We are right, then, in greeting the rejuvenescent summer with devout faith and hope. Below the surface din and clashing of the struggle for life we hear the undertone of the deep ethical purpose, as it rolls in solemn music through the ages, its volume swelled by every victory, great or small, of right over wrong, till in the fullness of time, in God's own time, it shall burst forth in the triumphant chorus of Humanity purified and redeemed.

WEALTH*

Andrew Carnegie

The problem of our age is the proper administration of wealth, so that the ties of brotherhood may still bind together the rich and poor in harmonious relationship. The conditions of human life have not only been changed, but revolutionized, within the past few

---

*From the *North American Review,* 148 (1889), pp. 653–64.

hundred years. In former days there was little difference between the dwelling, dress, food, and environment of the chief and those of his retainers. The Indians are to-day where civilized man then was. When visiting the Sioux, I was led to the wigwam of the chief. It was just like the others in external appearance, and even within the difference was trifling between it and those of the poorest of his braves. The contrast between the palace of the millionaire and the cottage of the laborer with us to-day measures the change which has come with civilization.

This change, however, is not to be deplored, but welcomed as highly beneficial. It is well, nay, essential for the progress of the race, that the houses of some should be homes for all that is highest and best in literature and the arts, and for all the refinements of civilization, rather than that none should be so. Much better this great irregularity than universal squalor. Without wealth there can be no Mæcenas. The "good old times" were not good old times. Neither master nor servant was as well situated then as to-day. A relapse to old conditions would be disastrous to both—not the least so to him who serves—and would sweep away civilization with it. But whether the change be for good or ill, it is upon us, beyond our power to alter, and therefore to be accepted and made the best of. It is a waste of time to criticize the inevitable.

It is easy to see how the change has come. One illustration will serve for almost every phase of the cause. In the manufacture of products we have the whole story. It applies to all combinations of human industry, as stimulated and enlarged by the inventions of this scientific age. Formerly articles were manufactured at the domestic hearth or in small shops which formed part of the household. The master and his apprentices worked side by side, the latter living with the master, and therefore subject to the same conditions. When these apprentices rose to be masters, there was little or no change in their mode of life, and they, in turn, educated in the same routine succeeding apprentices. There was, substantially, social equality, and even political equality, for those engaged in industrial pursuits had then little or no political voice in the State.

But the inevitable result of such a mode of manufacture was crude articles at high prices. To-day the world obtains commodities of excellent quality at prices which even the generation preceding this would have deemed incredible. In the commercial world similar causes have produced similar results, and the race is benefited thereby. The poor enjoy what the rich could not before afford. What were the luxuries have become the necessaries of life. The laborer has now more comforts than the farmer had a few generations ago. The farmer has more luxuries than the landlord had, and is more richly clad and better housed. The landlord has books and pictures rarer, and appointments more artistic, than the King could then obtain.

The price we pay for this salutary change is, no doubt, great. We assemble thousands of operatives in the factory, in the mine, and in the counting-house, of whom the employer can know little or nothing, and to whom the employer is little better than a myth. All intercourse between them is at an end. Rigid Castes are formed, and, as usual, mutual ignorance breeds mutual distrust. Each Caste is without sympathy for the other, and ready to credit anything disparaging in regard to it. Under the law of competition, the employer of thousands is forced into the strictest economies, among which the rates paid to labor figure prominently, and often there is friction between the employer and the employed, between capital and labor, between rich and poor. Human society loses homogeneity.

The price which society pays for the law of competition, like the price it pays for cheap comforts and luxuries, is also great; but the advantages of this law are also greater still, for it is to this law that we owe our wonderful material development, which brings improved conditions in its train. But, whether the law be benign or not, we must say of it, as we say of the change in the conditions of men to which we have referred: It is here; we cannot evade it; no substitutes for it have been found; and while the law may be sometimes hard for the individual, it is best for the race, because it insures the survival of the fittest in every department. We accept and welcome, therefore, as conditions to which we must accommodate ourselves, great inequality of environment, the concentration of business, industrial and commercial, in the hands of a few, and the law of competition between these, as being not only beneficial, but essential for the future progress of the race. Having accepted these, it follows that there must be great scope for the exercise of special ability in the merchant and in the manufacturer who has to conduct affairs upon a great scale. That this talent for organization and management is rare among men is proved by the fact that it invariably secures for its possessor enormous rewards, no matter where or under what laws or conditions. The experienced in affairs always rate the MAN whose services can be obtained as a partner as not only the first consideration, but such as to render the question of his capital scarcely worth considering, for such men soon create capital; while, without the special talent required, capital soon takes wings. Such men become interested in firms or corporations using millions; and estimating only simple interest to be made upon the capital invested, it is inevitable that their income must exceed their expenditures, and that they must accumulate wealth. Nor is there any middle ground which such men can occupy, because the great manufacturing or commercial concern which does not earn at least interest upon its capital soon becomes bankrupt. It must either go forward or fall behind: to stand still is impossible. It is a condition essential for its successful operation that it should be thus far profitable, and even that, in addition to interest on capital, it should make profit. It is a law, as certain as any of the others named, that men possessed of this peculiar talent for affairs, under the free play of economic forces, must, of necessity, soon be in receipt of more revenue than can be judiciously expended upon themselves; and this law is as beneficial for the race as the others.

Objections to the foundations upon which society is based are not in order, because the condition of the race is better with these than it has been with any others which have been tried. Of the effect of any new substitutes proposed we cannot be sure. The Socialist or Anarchist who seeks to overturn present conditions is to be regarded as attacking the foundation upon which civilization itself rests, for civilization took its start from the day that the capable, industrious workman said to his incompetent and lazy fellow, "If thou dost not sow, thou shalt not reap," and thus ended primitive Communism by separating the drones from the bees. One who studies this subject will soon be brought face to face with the conclusion that upon the sacredness of property civilization itself depends—the right of the laborer to his hundred dollars in the savings bank, and equally the legal right of the millionaire to his millions. To those who propose to substitute Communism for this intense Individualism the answer, therefore, is: The race has tried that. All progress from that barbarous day to the present time has resulted from its displacement. Not evil, but good, has come to the race from the accumulation of wealth by those who have the ability and energy that produce it. But even if we admit for a moment that it might be better for the race to discard its present foundation, Individualism,—that it is a nobler ideal that man should labor, not for himself alone, but in and for a brotherhood of his fellows, and share with them all in common ... —even admit all this, and a sufficient answer is, This is not evolution, but revolution. It necessitates the changing of human nature itself—a work of aeons, even if it were good to change it, which we cannot know. It is not practicable in our day or in our age. Even if desirable theoretically, it belongs to another and long-succeeding sociological stratum. Our duty is with what is practicable now; with the next step possible in our day and generation. It is criminal to waste our energies in endeavoring to uproot, when all we can profitably or possibly accomplish is to bend the universal tree of humanity a little in the direction most favorable to the production of good fruit under existing circumstances. We might as well urge the destruction of the highest existing type of man because he failed to reach our ideal as to favor the destruction of Individualism, Private Property, the Law of Accumulation of Wealth, and the Law of Competition; for these are the highest results of human experience, the soil in which society so far has produced the best fruit. Unequally or unjustly, perhaps, as these laws sometimes operate, and imperfect as they appear to the Idealist, they are, nevertheless, like the highest type of man, the best and most valuable of all that humanity has yet accomplished.

We start, then, with a condition of affairs under which the best interests of the race are promoted, but which inevitably gives wealth to the few. Thus far, accepting conditions as they exist, the situation can be surveyed and pronounced good. The question then arises,—and, if the foregoing be correct, it is the only question with which we have to deal,—What is the proper mode of administering wealth after the laws upon which civilization is founded have thrown it into the hands of the few? And it is of this great question that I believe I offer the true solution. It will be understood that *fortunes* are here spoken of, not moderate sums saved by many years of effort, the returns from which are required for the comfortable maintenance and education of families. This is not *wealth*, but only *competence*, which it should be the aim of all to acquire.

There are but three modes in which surplus wealth can be disposed of. It can be left to the families of the decedents; or it can be bequeathed for public purposes: or, finally, it can be administered during their lives by its possessors. Under the first and second modes most of the wealth of the world that has reached the few has hitherto been applied. Let us in turn consider each of these modes. The first is the most injudicious. In monarchical countries, the estates and the greatest portion of the wealth are left to the first son, that the vanity of the parent may be gratified by the thought that his name and title are to descend to succeeding generations unimpaired. The condition of this class in Europe to-day teaches the futility of such hopes or ambitions. The successors have become impoverished through their follies or from the fall in the value of land. Even in Great Britain the strict law of entail has been found inadequate to maintain the status of an hereditary class. Its soil is rapidly passing into the hands of the stranger. Under republican institutions the division of property among the children is much fairer, but the question which forces itself upon thoughtful men in all lands is: Why should men leave great fortunes to their children? If this is done from affection, is it not misguided affection? Observation teaches that, generally speaking, it is not well for the children that they should be so burdened. Neither is it well for the state. Beyond providing for the wife and daughters moderate sources of income, and very moderate allowances indeed, if any, for the sons, men may well hesitate, for it is no longer questionable that great sums bequeathed oftener work more for the injury than for the good of the recipients. Wise men will soon conclude that, for the best interests of the members of their families and of the state, such bequests are an improper use of their means. . . . The thoughtful man must shortly say, "I would as soon leave to my son a curse as the almighty dollar," and admit to himself that it is not the welfare of the children, but family pride, which inspires these enormous legacies.

As to the second mode, that of leaving wealth at death for public uses, it may be said that this is only a means for the disposal of wealth, provided a man is content to wait until he is dead before it becomes of much good in the world. Knowledge of the results of legacies bequeathed is not calculated to inspire the brightest hopes of much posthumous good being accomplished. The cases are not few in which the real object sought by the testator is not attained, nor are they few in which his real wishes are thwarted. In many cases the bequests are so used as to become only monuments of his folly. It is well to remember that it requires the exercise of not less ability than that which acquired the wealth to use it so as to be really beneficial to the community. Besides this, it may fairly be said that no man is to be extolled for doing what he cannot help doing, nor is he to be thanked by the community to which he only leaves wealth at death. Men who leave vast sums in this way may fairly be thought men who would not have left it at all, had they been able to take it with them. The memories of such cannot be held in grateful remembrance, for there is no grace in their gifts. It is not to be wondered at that such bequests seem so generally to lack the blessing. . . .

There remains, then, only one mode of using great fortunes;

but in this we have the true antidote for the temporary unequal distribution of wealth, the reconciliation of the rich and the poor—a reign of harmony—another ideal, differing, indeed, from that of the Communist in requiring only the further evolution of existing conditions, not the total overthrow of our civilization. It is founded upon the present most intense individualism, and the race is prepared to put it in practice by degrees whenever it pleases. Under its sway we shall have an ideal state, in which the surplus wealth of the few will become, in the best sense, the property of the many, because administered for the common good, and this wealth, passing through the hands of a few, can be made a much more potent force for the elevation of our race than if it had been distributed in small sums to the people themselves. Even the poorest can be made to see this, and to agree that great sums gathered by some of their fellow-citizens and spent for public purposes, from which the masses reap the principal benefit, are more valuable to them than if scattered among them through the course of many years in trifling amounts. . . .

Poor and restricted are our opportunities in this life; narrow our horizon; our best work most imperfect; but rich men should be thankful for one inestimable boon. They have it in their power during their lives to busy themselves in organizing benefactions from which the masses of their fellows will derive lasting advantage, and thus dignify their own lives. The highest life is probably to be reached, not by such imitation of the life of Christ as Count Tolstoi* gives us, but, while animated by Christ's spirit, by recognizing the changed conditions of this age, and adopting modes of expressing this spirit suitable to the changed conditions under which we live; still laboring for the good of our fellows, which was the essence of his life and teaching, but laboring in a different manner.

This, then, is held to be the duty of the man of Wealth: First, to set an example of modest, unostentatious living, shunning display or extravagance; to provide moderately for the legitimate wants of those dependent upon him; and after doing so to consider all surplus revenues which come to him simply as trust funds, which he is called upon to administer, and strictly bound as a matter of duty to administer in the manner which, in his judgment, is best calcu-

---

*[Editor's note: Count Tolstoi: Leo Tolstoi (1828-1910), a Russian writer, author of *War and Peace*, who late in life became a religious philosopher. One of his ethical teachings was that property is the principal source of evil in men, a doctrine obviously at odds with Carnegie's own "gospel."]

lated to produce the most beneficial results for the community—the man of wealth thus becoming the mere agent and trustee for his poorer brethren, bringing to their service his superior wisdom, experience, and ability to administer, doing for them better than they would or could do for themselves. . . .

The best uses to which surplus wealth can be put have already been indicated. Those who would administer wisely must, indeed, be wise, for one of the serious obstacles to the improvement of our race is indiscriminate charity. It were better for mankind that the millions of the rich were thrown into the sea than so spent as to encourage the slothful, the drunken, the unworthy. Of every thousand dollars spent in so called charity to-day, it is probable that $950 is unwisely spent; so spent, indeed, as to produce the very evils which it proposes to mitigate or cure. A well-known writer of philosophic books admitted the other day that he had given a quarter of a dollar to a man who approached him as he was coming to visit the house of his friend. He knew nothing of the habits of this beggar; knew not the use that would be made of this money, although he had every reason to suspect that it would be spent improperly. This man professed to be a disciple of Herbert Spencer; yet the quarter-dollar given that night will probably work more injury than all the money which its thoughtless donor will ever be able to give in true charity will do good. He only gratified his own feelings, saved himself from annoyance,—and this was probably one of the most selfish and very worst actions of his life, for in all respects he is most worthy.

In bestowing charity, the main consideration should be to help those who will help themselves; to provide part of the means by which those who desire to improve may do so; to give those who desire to rise the aids by which they may rise; to assist, but rarely or never to do all. Neither the individual nor the race is improved by alms-giving. Those worthy of assistance, except in rare cases, seldom require assistance. The really valuable men of the race never do, except in cases of accident or sudden change. Every one has, of course, cases of individuals brought to his own knowledge where temporary assistance can do genuine good, and these he will not overlook. But the amount which can be wisely given by the individual for individuals is necessarily limited by his lack of knowledge of the circumstances connected with each. He is the only true reformer who is as careful and as anxious not to aid the unworthy as he is to aid the worthy, and, perhaps, even more so, for in alms-giving more injury is probably done by rewarding vice than by relieving virture. . . .

Thus is the problem of Rich and Poor to be solved. The laws of accumulation will be left free; the laws of distribution free. Individualism will continue, but the millionaire will be but a trustee for the poor; intrusted for a season with a great part of the increased wealth of the community, but administering it for the community far better than it could or would have done for itself. The best minds will thus have reached a stage in the development of the race in which it is clearly seen that there is no mode of disposing of surplus wealth creditable to thoughtful and earnest men into whose hands it flows save by using it year by year for the general good. This day already dawns. But a little while, and although, without incurring the pity of their fellows, men may die sharers in great business enterprises from which their capital cannot be or has not been withdrawn, and is left chiefly at death for public uses, yet the man who dies leaving behind him millions of available wealth, which was his to administer during life, will pass away "unwept, unhonored, and unsung," no matter to what uses he leaves the dross which he cannot take with him. Of such as these the public verdict will then be: "The man who dies thus rich dies disgraced."

Such, in my opinion, is the true Gospel concerning Wealth, obedience to which is destined some day to solve the problem of the Rich and the Poor, and to bring "Peace on earth, among men Good-Will."

A SHORT HISTORY OF ANGLO–SAXON FREEDOM*

James K. Hosmer

On the 30th of April, 1789, Washington, as the first President of the United States, took a solemn oath to maintain the Federal Constitution. . . . As Washington took the oath, the pulsations began of the mighty engine whose accomplishment through the hundred years need not here be rehearsed. Government of the people, by the people, and for the people, went into operation,—a thing at that time unknown elsewhere among civilized nations.

Unknown elsewhere; but had the world never before seen

*From James K. Hosmer, *A Short History of Anglo-Saxon Freedom* (New York: Charles Scribner's Sons, 1890), pp. 1–11, 308–11, 322–25.

anything like it? As a polity, it was no original device, but a revival of something most ancient. I once crossed the North Sea, and coming upon deck after a night of storm, found the ship entering a great river, out from which rolled masses of ice. From the deck a monotonous, far-extending landscape could be seen, dotted here and there with compact red-roofed villages. Once landed, it was a journey of many leagues before the broad plains were left behind, and we reached a country more picturesque. If, however, the plains near the mouths of the rivers Weser and Elbe offer little attraction to the eye, no land is more interesting through its associations to the mind; for here lay the primeval home of the Angles and Saxons, with their kindred, the Jutes, just north, the remote forefathers of the imperial race which, now one hundred and twenty millions strong, retains substantially the language, institutions, and blood of those ancestors after the lapse of nearly two thousand years. In the ancient villages we can see distinctly a life proceeding, in some of its features, similar to that of English-speaking men at the present hour.

The forefathers were not utter savages. Although fierce fighters, they were at the same time busy fishermen and farmers. Though hard drinkers, the scenes within their homes were often not without a simple dignity, as the earl's wife with a troop of maidens bore the bowl of ale or mead about the hall while the minstrels sang. They possessed the runic alphabet, and showed in dress and arms an appreciation of the beautiful. The freeman in times that soon follow wore a smock-frock of coarse linen or wool falling to his knees, identical almost with that of the modern English ploughman. While it was the common garb of all classes, it was among those of good station handsomely embroidered: about feet and legs were wound linen bands, parti-colored. In winter, a hood covered the head, and over the shoulders was thrown a blue cloak, sometimes fastened by a costly clasp. For their constant warfare, the coats of ringed mail that were necessary, the swords scored with mystic runes while the hilts were finely wrought in silver and bronze, the helmets with heads of boars, wolves, or falcons for crests,—all made plain the skill of the smiths. In the society all the *eeorls*, or land-owning freemen, stood equal; they were bound together in families in such a way that if one underwent an injury, all his kin lay under obligation to exact reparation; as also they lay under obligation to afford reparation, if one of their number had inflicted the injury. Each clan occupied its own *mark*, or village, a tract held by the occupiers in common. The homesteads within the *tun* (the stockade, quickset hedge, or protecting circle of earth) were held in severalty, modified, however, by a reservation of public rights; but the pasture and forest, stretching far, since wealth lay largely in flocks and herds, and since a good provision of wood was necessary for the winter, were free to all inhabitants. Between the homesteads, on the one hand, and the pasture and forest, on the other, was land the tenure of which was intermediate in its character. Such was the plough-land upon which each eeorl raised food for his household and cattle, but was under restrictions imposed by the community; such, too, was the meadow, which individuals owned from early spring to the time of the hay-harvest, but which through fall and winter was common feeding-ground for the swine and kine of all. . . .

In the centre of the tun was the *moot-hill*, or perhaps a great tree, where the freemen came together to deliberate and to govern themselves. Here was administered the business of the common pasture and forest; here the grass-land was portioned out in the early spring, and the plough-land equably allotted. In case of a change in the private holding, the seller handed to the buyer a turf or a twig cut on the ground in question, in token of the transfer. As time proceeded, the tie of kinship gave way to the tie of neighborhood, but the customs did not change. As to the territory, there remained the individual holding, the common, and the land held by intermediate tenure; as to the people, eeorl, laet, theow, aetheling, retained each his place. Above all, the moot remained the centre of life in the mark. It is probable, too, that here took place, after matters peculiar to the little community were disposed of, the choosing of the representatives, who were to speak for those who sent them in the larger moots of the *hundred* and the *folc*.

For before history begins, a series of moots ranging upward from the assembly of the mark in ever-widening comprehensiveness had come to pass. Marks were gathered into hundreds, districts sending, each, perhaps, one hundred men to war; and these again into the great tribe, or folc. Each division had its proper moot, the marks appearing probably by their representatives in the higher moots. On great occasions, and also at stated times, as at the solstice, the freemen gathered in thousands to the great *folc-moot*, dispensing with representation. The priests proclaimed silence and maintained order. Speakers were at liberty to persuade, but no one had power to command. The nation, which, upon occasion, became at once a military host, sometimes opposed by loud shouts, some-times approved by shaking their spears, while in vehement moments they clashed together weapon and shield. No functionary was recognized, except as he was elected by the national voice. No one was King, except as his title was based on the suffrages of the freemen. . . .

Let us now set side by side ancient Germany and modern America, the ancient prolific mother and the youngest child; though the points of contrast are marked enough, the points of resemblance will be found at the same time numerous and striking. A nation of sixty millions is vastly different from a tribe of a few thousands; the elaborate civilization of the nineteenth century is vastly different from the culture scarcely raised above barbarism, of the first; the intricate enginery of peace and war, the cities of iron and granite, the network of conventionalities by which we are bound, are far removed from the simple spear and shield, the palisaded tun, and the artless etiquette of the hall of the aetheling. Here are points, nevertheless, in which we agree with those men of the past. . . . The American citizen, sovereign in all his privileges, is the counterpart of the eeorl, except that a share in the ownership of land is no longer a condition of the franchise. In the definite subordination, moreover, of tun to hundred, of hundred to shire, and of shire to tribe, we have no remote foreshadowing of town, county, state, and federal union. The New England town-meeting is the moot of the Anglo-Saxon tun, resuscitated with hardly a circumstance of difference; as closely parallel, perhaps, also are the ancient moots of the shire, if they were constituted of the representatives from each tithing, to the county boards of the Northwest made up by the supervisors of the different townships. Representation, the principle that pervades the whole apparatus for law-making and administration in the higher ranges of politics, is distinctly an Anglo-Saxon idea, proceeding probably from the earliest times. . . .

Our freedom, then, is no new thing, but developed from the ancient Anglo-Saxon freedom, something transmitted from times perhaps prehistoric. We are to trace its course through nearly two thousand years, from the German plains to the United States of to-day. The fluctuations in its history have been extreme and constant. Many times it has been upon the verge of extinction. Always, however, it has been maintained, until at the present hour it advances to the dominion of the world. . . .

Though Anglo-Saxon freedom in a more or less partial form has been adopted (it would be better perhaps to say imitated) by every nation in Europe, but Russia, and in Asia by Japan, the hopes for that freedom, in the future, rest with the English-speaking race. By that race alone it has been preserved amidst a thousand perils; to that race alone is it thoroughly congenial; if we can conceive the possibility of the disappearance among peoples of that race, the chance would be small for that freedom's survival. They are the Levites to whom, in especial, is committed the guardianship of this ark, so infinitely precious to the world. In no century of its career has the band understood so well the sacred character of its responsibility, and looked with such love upon the trust it was appointed to defend.

A pamphlet widely circulated during the past decade contemplates the future of the English-speaking race and their institutions with still more enthusiasm. In a hundred years, says [its author, F. Barham] Zincke, the United States will have a population of 800,000,000; Canada, 64,000,000; Australia, 48,000,000; South Africa, 16,000,000; Great Britain and Ireland, 70,000,000: altogether, in his estimate, there will be 1,000,000,000, substantially the same in language, institutions and ideals. The United States will have overflowed southward and into the islands of the Pacific. Our limits will touch those of Australia and New Zealand, which on their side, too, will flow out. In South Africa, also, the "Englishry" will have wonderfully multiplied and poured into the regions lying northward, which Livingstone and Stanley have laid open and are proving to be habitable. The flower of the species, therefore, says the writer, who has no mean idea of our stock, will have come, in the course of a century, to occupy the fairest parts of the planet. What will be the nature of the society which one hundred years from now will be thus widespread? It will be fundamentally the same in manners and ideas, with slight differences due to climate and soil. . . . There will be few savages, no serfs, or slaves,—not many drones or Sybarites, —none without civilization. All will be able to read and write, have homes of their own, hold enough land to yield to intelligent industry a good support. They will have no social or political superiors; they will manage for themselves their own business,—Abraham Lincoln's "government of the people, by the people, and for the people." Society, legislation, administration of affairs, will be to them a most effective means of education. At the head of all, though not necessarily in one nationality with the rest, will stand the United States, our President the foremost man. . . .

America is no less beset with questions of difficulty peculiar to herself. What does justice to the negro demand, and how shall it be secured to him, while at the same time our institutions are held safe,—institutions which presuppose as a first condition of their existence that an intelligent people shall administer them? Can the civil service be reformed, and legislatures, State and Federal, be redeemed from corruption and inefficiency? What safeguards can be thrown about the public schools, indispensable cradles of good citizenship, institutions of fundamental importance, at no time in our history too zealously cherished, and at the present hour boldly attacked by the power which so often has been the most formidable foe of freedom? What dikes can be erected against the undesirable foreign flood, which, pouring in yearly in volume always increasing through the unobstructed sluices of our seaports, seems likely so far to dilute our blood as to make it unequal to the task of sustaining Anglo-Saxon freedom? ... Meantime, the flood ever rises: through the sluices pour currents from a score of peoples, the stream often noisome through ignorance and vice. No fact is better established than that strains of men, as of the lower animals, are improved by crossing. To breed in and in produces degeneration. New blood, provided it comes from sources not too remote, and is without morbid taint, invigorates. New blood is to be welcomed, and yet it should not be infused to so large an extent as to make of the strain a different thing. Anglo-Saxon we ought to remain, if Anglo-Saxon freedom is to be maintained. "It is part of the inexorable logic of fact and nature, that you cannot have the growth of the living creature, plant, animal, man, nation, seriously injured in the growing time and then set right in subsequent years. The stunted tree, the starved child, the crushed and spirit-broken nation, bear the marks of their injury to the end." As regards political freedom, every people but the Anglo-Saxons has been at some time crushed and become spirit-broken. To Anglo-Saxons alone can our American freedom be safely intrusted.

ADOLESCENT GIRLS AND THEIR EDUCATION*

Granville Stanley Hall

Our modern knowledge of woman represents her as having characteristic differences from man in every organ and tissue, as conservative in body and mind, fulfilling the function of seeing to it that no acquired good be lost to mankind, ... as normally representing childhood and youth in the full meridian of its glory in all her

---

*From *Adolescence* (New York: Appleton, 1904), pp. 561–62, 609–12, 627–28, 646.

dimensions and nature so that she is at the top of the human curve from which the higher super-man of the future is to evolve. . . . Her whole soul, conscious and unconscious, is best conceived as a magnificent organ of heredity, and to its laws all her psychic activities, if unperverted, are true. She is by nature more typical and a better representative of the race and less prone to specialization. Her peculiar organs, while constituting a far larger proportion of her body than those of man, are hidden and their psychic reverberations are dim, less localized, more all-pervasive. She works by intuition and feeling; fear, anger, pity, love, and most of the emotions have a wider range and greater intensity. If she abandons her natural naïveté and takes up the burden of guiding and accounting for her life by consciousness, she is likely to lose more than she gains, according to the old saw that she who deliberates is lost. Secondary, tertiary, and quaternary sex qualities are developed far beyond her ken or that of science, in a way that the latter is only beginning to glimpse. While she needs tension that only the most advanced modern psychology sees to be sexual at root, we shall never know the true key to her nature until we understand how the nest and the cradle are larger wombs; the home, a larger nest; the tribe, state, church, and school, larger homes and irradiations from it. Biological psychology already dreams of a new philosophy of sex which places the wife and mother at the heart of a new world and makes her the object of a new religion and almost of a new worship, that will give her reverent exemption from sex competition and reconsecrate her to the higher responsibilities of the human race, into the past and future of which the roots of her being penetrate; where the blind worship of mere mental illumination has no place; and where her real superiority to man will have free course and be glorified and the ideals of the old matriarchates again find embodiment in fit and due degree. . . .

Excessive intellectualism insidiously instils the same aversion to "brute maternity" as does luxury, overindulgence, or excessive devotion to society. Just as man must fight the battles of competition, and be ready to lay down his life for his country, so woman needs a heroism of her own to face the pain, danger, and work of bearing and rearing children, and whatever lowers the tone of her body, nerves, or *morale* so that she seeks to escape this function, merits the same kind of opprobrium which society metes out to the exempts who can not or who will not fight to save their country in time of need. In an ideal and progressive state those exempted from this function would be at the bottom among those least fitted to survive, but where the birth-rate goes down in proportion to intelligence and education, either the principle of the survival of the best is false or else these classes are not the best, or are impaired by their training or environment. While we need not consider the cranky and extreme left wing of this movement, which strives to theoretically ignore and practically escape the monthly function, or the several coteries of half-cultured scientific women, personally known to the writer, who devote time, money, and effort to investigating artificial methods of gestation, . . . we find wide-spread among the most cultured classes the one or two child system which would atone for numbers by lavishing wealth and even care to safeguard and bring the few to the highest possible development. But only children are usually twice spoiled—first by enfeebled heredity at birth, and second by excessive care and indulgence. . . . The enfeebled nature of only children often needs exceptional incubating all through childhood and youth, but with the decline of reproductive vigor not only the wise neglect but the sound motherly good sense in treatment is prone also to lapse toward the senile and grandmotherly overfostering, so that partial sterility always involves the danger of perverted motherly instincts. From a biological point of view, there is an unutterable depth of pathos in the almost morbid oversolicitude of the invalid and highly educated mother for an only child to whom she has transmitted her enfeebled existence, and among the decadent families of New England this spectacle is not infrequent.

As Augustine said, the soul is made for God and is not happy till it finds rest in him, so woman's body and soul are made for maternity and she can never find true repose for either without it. The more we know of the contents of the young woman's mind the more clearly we see that everything conscious and unconscious in it points to this as the true goal of the way of life. Even if she does not realize it, her whole nature demands first of all children to love, who depend on her for care, and perhaps a little less, a man whom she heartily respects and trusts to strengthen and perhaps protect her in discharging this function. This alone can complete her being, and without it her sphere, however she shape it, is but a hemisphere; she is a little *détraqué*, and her destiny is more or less disarticulated from her inmost and deepest nature. All ripe, healthful, and womanly women desire this, and if they attain true self-knowledge confess it to themselves, however loath they may be to do so to others, and some who attain it too late wear their lives out in regret. Nothing can ever quite take its place, without it they are never completely happy, and every other satisfaction is a little vicarious. To see this is simple common sense and to admit it only common honesty. In an ideal society, with ideal men in it, woman's education should focus on motherhood and wifehood, and seek in every way to magnify these functions and to invest them with honor.

But the world is not right, and this career is not always optimal. Man is not always manly, but prone to be selfish and even sensuous, and so woman must strive to make the best of the second best. . . . This by no means signifies that every woman who takes to other absorbing pursuits has been disappointed. Happily for her, perhaps she often does not know her true rights but misconstrues them. She often loses a little light-heartedness, but is not consciously, or it may be even unconsciously, wearing off heartache. She feels a little lack of purpose. She had tasted adoration and felt her womanhood a noble thing, and in its place comes a little distrust, her self-respect is not quite so invincible, and she catches herself at self-justification that she is unwed. Her yesterdays seem a little dusty and her to-morrows a trifle faded. She craves something different and afar, and drags her anchor and perhaps slips adrift. Her joy in the many substitutes provided for her true happiness is nervously intense, yet she is harder to please and feels a trifle at odds with the world. As the years pass she perhaps grows fastidious and lavishes care upon herself, her regimen and toilet, and becomes, what I believe there is justification for calling, overcleanly in her person and all its surroundings. . . . She craves the costly; if unoccupied, grows inactive, luxurious, capricious, and freaky even in appetite, or gives herself up to Vanity Fair and develops a peculiar Americanized type, or else, in store or office, goes a trifle off in dress or form. Her disposition sags from its wonted buoyancy and the haze of ill health slowly gathers in her horizon. Her opinion of men is less favorable, and she perhaps at last falls a conscious prey to the gospel of the feminists, and learns that for ages woman was a drudge and man a brute whom women should now rise and subdue or at least insist for herself on all his rights and positions.

Fortunately few and now ever fewer reach this extreme. Among the greatest achievements of our race, I esteem the work of woman, largely in the last generation or two, in working out manifold new careers for herself, wherein those whom men exclude from it can rebuild so fair a substitute for their original Eden. So happy can the unwed now be in self-supporting vocations of charity, teaching, art, literature, religious and social vocations, and lighter manual callings requiring skill, fidelity, taste, in many of which lines she naturally excels man, that she finds not only consolation but content and joy. Here she is making the best possible original solution of her great problems, imposed on her by existing conditions, while many declared she could never do so, and no lover of his kind can fail to bid her so hearty a godspeed in all these endeavors. Those who see most clearly that bad conditions have forced her to compromise with her ideals, most fervently trust that her success in so doing may never make them forgotten. . . .

To be a true woman means to be yet more mother than wife. The madonna conception expresses man's highest comprehension of woman's real nature. Sexual relations are brief, but love and care of offspring are long. The elimination of maternity is one of the great calamities, if not diseases, of our age. . . . Art again to-day gives woman a waspish waist with no abdomen, as if to carefully score away every trace of her mission; usually with no child in her arms or even in sight; a mere figurine, calculated perhaps to entice, but not to bear; incidentally degrading the artist who depicts her to a fashion-plate painter, perhaps with suggestions of the arts of toilet, cosmetics, and coquetry, as if to promote decadent reaction to decadent stimuli. As in the Munchausen tale, the wolf slowly ate the running nag from behind until he found himself in the harness, so in the disoriented woman the mistress, virtuous and otherwise, is slowly supplanting the mother. Please she must, even though she can not admire, and can so easily despise men who can not lead her, although she become thereby lax and vapid.

The more exhausted men become, whether by overwork, unnatural city life, alcohol, recrudescent polygamic inclinations, exclusive devotion to greed and pelf; whether they become weak, stooping, blear-eyed, bald-headed, bow-legged, thin-shanked, or gross, coarse, barbaric, and bestial, the more they lose the power to lead woman or to arouse her nature, which is essentially passive. Thus her perversions are his fault. Man, before he lost the soil and piety, was not only her protector and provider, but her priest. He not only supported and defended, but inspired the souls of women, so admirably calculated to receive and elaborate suggestions, but not to originate them. In their inmost soul even young girls often experience disenchantment, find men little and no heroes, and so cease to revere and begin to think stupidly of them as they think coarsely of her. Sometimes the girlish conceptions of men are too romantic and exalted; often the intimacy of school and college wear off a charm, while man must not forget that to-day he too often fails to realize the just and legitimate expectations and ideals of women. If women confide themselves, body and soul, less to him than he desires, it is not she, but he, who is often chiefly to blame. Indeed, in some psychic respects it seems as if in human society the processes of subordinating the male to the female, carried so far in some of the animal species, had already begun. If he is not worshiped as formerly, it is because he is less worshipful or more effeminate, less vigorous and less able to excite and retain the great love of true, not to say great, women. . . .

As a psychologist, penetrated with the growing sense of the predominance of the heart over the mere intellect, I believe myself not alone in desiring to make a tender declaration of being more and more passionately in love with woman as I conceive she came from the hand of God. I keenly envy my Catholic friends their Maryolatry. Who ever asked if the holy mother, whom the wise men adored, knew the astronomy of the Chaldees or had studied Egyptian or Babylonian, or even whether she knew how to read or write her own tongue, and who has ever thought of caring? We can not conceive that she bemoaned any limitations of her sex, but she has been an object of adoration all these centuries because she glorified womanhood by being more generic, nearer the race, and richer in love, pity, unselfish devotion and intuition than man. The glorified madonna ideal shows us how much more whole and holy it is to be a woman than to be artist, orator, professor, or expert, and suggests to our own sex that to be a man is larger than to be gentleman, philosopher, general, president, or millionaire.

But with all this love and hunger in my heart, I can not help sharing in the growing fear that modern woman, at least in more ways and places than one, is in danger of declining from her orbit; that she is coming to lack just confidence and pride in her sex as such, and is just now in danger of lapsing to mannish ways, methods, and ideals, until her original divinity may become obscured.

SOCIOLOGY*

William Graham Sumner

Each of the sciences which, by giving to man greater knowledge of the laws of nature, has enabled him to cope more intelligently with

---

*From Albert Galloway Keller, ed., *War and Other Essays by William Graham Sumner* (New Haven: Yale University Press, 1913), pp. 167–92.

the ills of life, has had to fight for its independence of metaphysics. We have still lectures on metaphysical biology in some of our colleges and in some of our public courses, but biology has substantially won its independence.... Sociology, however, the latest of this series of sciences, is rather entering upon the struggle than emerging from it. Sociology threatens to withdraw an immense range of subjects of the first importance from the dominion of *a priori* speculation and arbitrary dogmatism, and the struggle will be severe in proportion to the dignity and importance of the subject....

Sociology is the science of life in society. It investigates the forces which come into action wherever a human society exists. It studies the structure and functions of the organs of human society, and its aim is to find out the laws in subordination to which human society takes its various forms and social institutions grow and change. Its practical utility consists in deriving the rules of right social living from the facts and laws which prevail by nature in the constitution and functions of society. It must, without doubt, come into collision with all other theories of right living which are founded on authority, tradition, arbitrary invention, or poetic imagination.

Sociology is perhaps the most complicated of all the sciences, yet there is no domain of human interest the details of which are treated ordinarily with greater facility. Various religions have various theories of social living, which they offer as authoritative and final.... Hence social problems and social phenomena present no difficulty to him who has only to cite an authority or obey a prescription.

Then again the novelists set forth "views" about social matters. To write and read novels is perhaps the most royal road to teaching and learning which has ever been devised. The proceeding of the novelists is kaleidoscopic. They turn the same old bits of colored glass over and over again into new combinations. There is no limit, no sequence, no bond of consistency. The romance-writing social philosopher always proves his case, just as a man always wins who plays chess with himself.

Then again the utopians and socialists make easy work of the complicated phenomena with which sociology has to deal. These persons, vexed with the intricacies of social problems and revolting against the facts of the social order, take upon themselves the task of inventing a new and better world. They brush away all which troubles us men and create a world free from annoying limitations and conditions—in their imagination. . . .

Then again all the whimsical people who have hobbies of one sort or another come forward with projects which are the result of a strong impression, an individual misfortune, or an unregulated benevolent desire, and which are therefore the product of a facile emotion, not of a laborious investigation.

Then again the *dilettanti* make light work of social questions. . . . A group of half-educated men may be relied upon to attack a social question and to hammer it dead in a few minutes with a couple of commonplaces and a sweeping *a priori* assumption. Above all other topics, social topics lend themselves to the purposes of the diner-out.

Two facts, however, in regard to social phenomena need only be mentioned to be recognized as true. (1) Social phenomena always present themselves to us in very complex combinations, and (2) it is by no means easy to interpret the phenomena. The phenomena are often at three or four removes from their causes. Tradition, prejudice, fashion, habit, and other similar obstacles continually warp and deflect the social forces, and they constitute interferences whose magnitude is to be ascertained separately for each case. It is also impossible for us to set up a social experiment. To do that we should need to dispose of the time and liberty of a certain number of men. It follows that sociology requires a special method, and that probably no science requires such peculiar skill and sagacity in the observer and interpreter of the phenomena which are to be studied. . . .

When, now, we take into account these difficulties and requirements, it is evident that the task of sociology is one which will call for especial and long training, and that it will probably be a long time yet before we can train up any body of special students who will be so well trained in the theory and science of society as to be able to form valuable opinions on points of social disease and social remedy. But it is a fact of familiar observation that all popular discussions of social questions seize directly upon points of social disease and social remedies. The diagnosis of some asserted social ill and the prescription of the remedy are undertaken offhand by the first comer, and without reflecting that the diagnosis of a social disease is many times harder than that of a disease in an individual, and that to prescribe for a society is to prescribe for an organism which is immortal. To err in prescribing for a man is at worst to kill him; to err in prescribing for a society is to set in operation injurious forces which extend, ramify, and multiply their effects in ever new combinations throughout an indefinite future. It may pay to experiment with an individual, because he cannot wait for medical science to be perfected; it cannot pay to experiment with a society, because the society does not die and can afford to wait. . . .

Social questions force themselves upon us in multitudes every year as our civilization advances and our society becomes complex. . . . The assumption which underlies almost all discussion of social topics is that we men need only to make up our minds what kind of a society we want to have, and that then we can devise means for calling that society into existence. It is assumed that we can decide to live on one spot of the earth's surface or another, and to pursue there one industry or another, and then that we can, by our devices, make that industry as productive as any other could be in that place. People believe that we have only to choose whether we will have aristocratic institutions or democratic institutions. It is believed that statesmen can, if they will, put a people in the way of material prosperity. It is believed that rent on land can be abolished if it is not thought expedient to have it. It is assumed that peasant proprietors can be brought into existence anywhere where it is thought that it would be an advantage to have them. These illustrations might be multiplied indefinitely. They show the need of sociology, and if we should go on to notice the general conceptions of society, its ills and their remedies, which are held by various religious, political, and social sects, we should find ample further evidence of this need.

Let us then endeavor to define the field of sociology. Life in society is the life of a human society on this earth. Its elementary conditions are set by the nature of human beings and the nature of the earth. We have already become familiar, in biology, with the transcendent importance of the fact that life on earth must be maintained by a struggle against nature, and also by a competition with other forms of life. In the latter fact biology and sociology touch. Sociology is a science which deals with one range of phenomena produced by the struggle for existence, while biology deals with another. The forces are the same, acting on different fields and under different conditions. The sciences are truly cognate. Nature contains certain materials which are capable of satisfying human needs, but those materials must, with rare and mean exceptions, be won by labor, and must be fitted to human use by more labor. As soon as any number of human beings are struggling each to win from nature the material goods necessary to support life, and are carrying on this struggle side by side, certain social forces come into operation. The prime condition of this society will lie in the ratio of its numbers to the supply of materials within its reach. For the supply at any moment attainable is an exact quantity, and the number of persons who can be supplied is arithmetically limited. If the actual number present is very much less than the number who might be supported, the condition of all must be ample and easy. Freedom and facility mark all social relations under such a state of things. If the number is larger than that which can be supplied, the condition of all must be one of want and distress, or else a few must be well provided, the others being proportionately still worse off. Constraint, anxiety, possibly tyranny and repression, mark social relations. It is when the social pressure due to an unfavorable ratio of population to land becomes intense that the social forces develop increased activity. Division of labor, exchange, higher social organization, emigration, advance in the arts, spring from the necessity of contending against the harsher conditions of existence which are continually reproduced as the population surpasses the means of existence on any given status.

The society with which we have to deal does not consist of any number of men. An army is not a society. A man with his wife and his children constitutes a society, for its essential parts are all present, and the number more or less is immaterial. A certain division of labor between the sexes is imposed by nature. The family as a whole maintains itself better under an organization with division of labor than it could if the functions were shared so far as possible. From this germ the development of society goes on by the regular steps of advancement to higher organization, accompanied and sustained by improvements in the arts. The increase of population goes on according to biological laws which are capable of multiplying the species beyond any assignable limits, so that the number to be provided for steadily advances and the status of ease and abundance gives way to a status of want and constraint. Emigration is the first and simplest remedy. . . . It is to be noticed, however, that emigration is painful to all men. To the uncivilized man, to emigrate means to abandon a mass of experiences and traditions which have been won by suffering, and to go out to confront new hardships and perils. To the civilized man migration means cutting off old ties of kin and country. The earth has been peopled by man at the cost of this suffering.

On the side of the land also stands the law of the diminishing return as a limitation. More labor gets more from the land, but not proportionately more. Hence, if more men are to be supported, there is need not of a proportionate increase of labor, but of a disproportionate increase of labor. The law of population, therefore, combined with the law of the diminishing returns, constitutes the great underlying condition of society. Emigration, improvements in the arts, in morals, in education, in political organization, are only stages in the struggle of man to meet these conditions, to break their force for a time, and to win room under them for ease and enlargement. Ease and enlargement mean either power to support more men on a given stage of comfort, or power to advance the comfort of a given number of men. Progress is a word which has no meaning save in view of the laws of population and the diminishing return, and it is quite natural that anyone who fails to understand those laws should fall into doubt which way progress points, whether towards wealth or poverty. The laws of population and the diminishing return, in their combination, are the iron spur which has driven the race on to all which it has ever achieved, and the fact that population ever advances, yet advances against a barrier which resists more stubbornly at every step of advance, unless it is removed to a new distance by some conquest of man over nature, is the guarantee that the task of civilization will never be ended, but that the need for more energy, more intelligence, and more virtue will never cease while the race lasts. If it were possible for an increasing population to be sustained by proportionate increments of labor, we should all still be living in the original home of the race on the spontaneous products of the earth. . . .

We have noticed that the relations involved in the struggle for existence are twofold. There is first the struggle of individuals to win the means of subsistence from nature, and secondly there is the competition of man with man in the effort to win a limited supply. The radical error of the socialists and sentimentalists is that they never distinguish these two relations from each other. They bring forward complaints which are really to be made, if at all, against the author of the universe for the hardships which man has to endure in his struggle with nature. The complaints are addressed, however, to society; that is, to other men under the same hardships. The only social element, however, is the competition of life, and when society is blamed for the ills which belong to the human lot, it is only burdening those who have successfully contended with those ills with the further task of conquering the same ills over again for somebody else. Hence liberty perishes in all socialistic schemes, and the tendency of such schemes is to the deterioration of society by burdening the good members and relieving the bad ones.

The law of the survival of the fittest was not made by man and cannot be abrogated by man. We can only, by interfering with it, produce the survival of the unfittest. If a man comes forward with any grievance against the order of society so far as this is shaped by human agency, he must have patient hearing and full redress; but if he addresses a demand to society for relief from the hardships of life, he asks simply that somebody else should get his living for him. In that case he ought to be left to find out his error from hard experience.

The sentimental philosophy starts from the first principle that nothing is true which is disagreeable, and that we must not believe anything which is "shocking," no matter what the evidence may be.... To this philosophy in all its grades the laws of population and the diminishing return have always been very distasteful. The laws which entail upon mankind an inheritance of labor cannot be acceptable to any philosophy which maintains that man comes into the world endowed with natural rights and an inheritor of freedom. It is a death-blow to any intuitional philosophy to find out, as an historical fact, what diverse thoughts, beliefs, and actions man has manifested, and it requires but little actual knowledge of human history to show that the human race has never had any ease which it did not earn, or any freedom which it did not conquer....

The whole retrospect of human history runs downwards towards beast-like misery and slavery to the destructive forces of nature. The whole history has been one series of toilsome, painful, and bloody struggles, first to find out where we were and what were the conditions of greater ease, and then to devise means to get relief. Most of the way the motives of advance have been experience of suffering and instinct. It is only in the most recent years that science has undertaken to teach without and in advance of suffering, and as yet science has to fight so hard against tradition that its authority is only slowly winning recognition....

As an illustration of the light which sociology throws on a great number of political and social phenomena which are constantly misconstrued, we may notice the differences in the industrial, political, and civil organizations which are produced all along at different stages of the ratio of population to land.

When a country is under-populated newcomers are not competitors, but assistants.... In such a state of things land is abundant and cheap. The possession of it confers no power or privilege. No one will work for another for wages when he can take up new land and be his own master. Hence it will pay no one to own more land than he can cultivate by his own labor, or with such aid as his own family supplies. Hence, again, land bears little or no rent; there will be no landlords living on rent and no laborers living on wages, but only a middle class of yeoman farmers. All are substantially on an equality, and democracy becomes the political form, because this is the only state of society in which the dogmatic assumption of equality, on which democracy is based, is realized as a fact. The same effects are powerfully reenforced by other facts. In a new and underpopulated country the industries which are most profitable are the extractive industries. The characteristic of these, with the exception of some kinds of mining, is that they call for only a low organization of labor and small amount of capital. Hence they allow the workman to become speedily his own master, and they educate him to freedom, independence, and self-reliance. At the same time, the social groups being only vaguely marked off from each other, it is easy to pass from one class of occupations, and consequently from one social grade, to another. Finally, under the same circumstances education, skill, and superior training have but inferior value compared with what they have in densely populated countries. The advantages lie, in an under-populated country, with the coarser, unskilled, manual occupations, and not with the highest developments of science, literature, and art.

If now we turn for comparison to cases of over-population we see that the struggle for existence and the competition of life are intense where the pressure of population is great. This competition draws out the highest achievements. It makes the advantages of capital, education, talent, skill, and training tell to the utmost. It draws out the social scale upwards and downwards to great extremes and produces aristocratic social organizations in spite of all dogmas of equality. Landlords, tenants (i.e., capitalist employers), and laborers are the three primary divisions of any aristocratic order, and they are sure to be developed whenever land bears rent and whenever tillage requires the application of large capital. At the same time liberty has to undergo curtailment. A man who has a square mile to himself can easily do as he likes, but a man who walks Broadway at noon or lives in a tenement-house finds his power to do as he likes limited by scores of considerations for the rights and feelings of his fellowmen. Furthermore, organization with subordination and discipline is essential in order that the society as a whole may win a support from the land. In an over-populated country the extremes of wealth and luxury are presented side by side with the extremes of poverty and distress. They are equally the products of an intense social pressure. The achievements of power are highest, the rewards of prudence, energy, enterprise, foresight, sagacity, and all other industrial virtues is greatest; on the other hand, the penalties of folly, weakness, error, and vice are most terrible. Pauperism, prostitution, and crime are the attendants of a state of society in which science, art, and literature reach their highest developments. Now it is evident that over-population and under-population are only relative terms. Hence as time goes on any under-populated nation is surely moving forward towards the other status, and is speedily losing its natural advantages which are absolute, and also that relative advantage which belongs to it if it is in neighborly relations with nations of dense population and high civilization; viz, the chance to borrow and assimilate from them the products, in arts and science, of high civilization without enduring the penalties of intense social pressure.

We have seen that if we should try by any measures of arbitrary interference and assistance to relieve the victims of social pressure from the calamity of their position we should only offer premiums to folly and vice and extend them further. We have also seen that we must go forward and meet our problems. We cannot escape them by running away. If then it be asked what the wit and effort of man can do to struggle with the problems offered by social pressure, the answer is that he can do only what his instinct has correctly and surely led him to do without any artificial social organization of any kind, and that is, by improvements in the arts, in science, in morals, in political institutions, to widen and strengthen the power of man over nature. The task of dealing with social ills is not a new task. People set about it and discuss it as if the human race had hitherto neglected it, and as if the solution of the problem was to be something new in form and substance, different from the solution of all problems which have hitherto engaged human effort. In truth, the human race has never done anything else but struggle with the problem of social welfare. That struggle constitutes history, or the life of the human race on earth. That struggle embraces all minor problems which occupy attention here, save those of religion, which reaches beyond this world and finds its objects beyond this life. Every successful effort to widen the power of man over nature is a real victory over poverty, vice, and misery, taking things in general and in the long run. It would be hard to find a single instance of a direct assault by positive effort upon poverty, vice, and misery which has not either failed or, if it has not failed directly and entirely, has not entailed other evils greater than the one which it removed. The only two things which really tell on the welfare of man on earth are hard work and self-denial (in technical language, labor and capital), and these tell most when they are brought to bear directly upon the effort to earn an honest living, to accumulate capital, and to bring up a family of children to be industrious and self-denying in their turn. I repeat that this is the way to work for the welfare of man on earth; and what I mean to say is that the common notion that when we are going to work for the social welfare of man we must adopt a great dogma, organize for the realization of some great scheme, have before us an abstract ideal, or otherwise do anything but live honest and industrious lives, is a great mistake. From the standpoint of the sociologist pessimism and optimism are alike impertinent. To be an optimist one must forget the frightful sanctions which are attached to the laws of right living. To be a pessimist one must overlook the education and growth which are the product of effort and self-denial. In either case one is passing judgment on what is inevitably fixed, and on which the approval or condemnation of man can produce no effect. The facts and laws are, once and for all, so, and for us men that is the end of the matter. The only persons for whom there would be any sense in the question whether life is worth living are primarily the yet unborn children, and secondarily the persons who are proposing to found families. For these latter the question would take a somewhat modified form: Will life be worth living for children born of me? This question is, unfortunately, not put to themselves by the appropriate persons as it would be if they had been taught sociology. The sociologist is often asked if he wants to kill off certain classes of troublesome and burdensome persons. No such inference follows from any sound sociological doctrine, but it is allowed to infer, as to a great many persons and classes, that it would have been better for society, and would have involved no pain to them, if they had never been born. . . .

The old classical civilization fell under an irruption of barbarians from without. It is possible that our new civilization may perish by an explosion from within. The sentimentalists have been preaching for a century notions of rights and equality, of the dignity, wisdom, and power of the proletariat, which have filled the minds of ignorant men with impossible dreams. The thirst for luxurious enjoyment has taken possession of us all. It is the dark side of the power to foresee a possible future good with such distinctness as to make it a motive of energy and persevering industry—a power which is distinctly modern. Now the thirst for luxurious enjoyment, when brought into connection with the notions of rights, of power, and of equality, and dissociated from the notions of industry and economy, produces the notion that a man is robbed of his rights if he has not everything that he wants, and that he is deprived of equality if he sees anyone have more than he has, and that he is a fool if, having the power of the State in his hands, he allows this state of things to last. Then we have socialism, communism, and nihilism; and the fairest conquests of civilization, with all their promise of solid good to man, on the sole conditions of virtue and wisdom, may be scattered to the winds in a war of classes, or trampled underfoot by a mob which can only hate what it cannot enjoy.

MIND AS A SOCIAL FACTOR*

Lester Ward

After many centuries of exclusive study of the soul, the thinkers of the world turned their attention for some centuries more to the study of the intellect. . . . At last there rose up the scientific philosophy which essayed to explain the nature of mind. . . . Mind was shown to be a function of body and psychology became a department of biology. Man has now taken his true position in the animal world as a product of development. Brain, which alone raises him above other animals, has been developed in the same manner as the other anatomical characters. The brain is the organ of the mind, its physical seat and cause. Mind is therefore a natural product of evolution, and its achievements are to be classed and studied along with all other natural phenomena. . . . The modern scientist places all objects in the midst of an infinite series of antecedents and consequents. . . . Mind itself is a link of this endless chain. . . .

The protracted study of nature's processes leads to admiration of them, and the belief has become prevalent that they are not only unalterable but also in some way necessarily beneficent. . . . Out of this earnest and laudable strife to discover the true method of nature has grown, logically enough, the assumption that when found it must be something of great worth. It is commonly supposed that the highest wisdom of man is to learn and then to follow

---

*From Ward, *Glimpses of the Cosmos* (3 vols.; New York: G. P. Putnam's Sons, 1913), Vol. III, pp. 361–77.

the ways of nature. Those dissatisfied people who would improve upon the natural course of events are rebuked as meddlers with the unalterable. Their systems are declared utopian, their laws *bruta fulmina*. All efforts in this direction are held to be trifling and are stigmatised as so many ignorant attempts to nullify the immutable laws of nature.

This general mode of reasoning is carried into all departments of human life. In government every attempt to improve the condition of the state is condemned and denounced. . . . In commerce and trade absolute freedom is insisted upon. . . . In social affairs these doctrines are carried to their extreme logical outcome. The laws of nature as they manifest themselves in society must be left wholly untouched. . . . Competition can be depended upon to correct abuses. The seller must be allowed to exaggerate and misstate the nature of his wares. This has the effect to sharpen the wits of the buyer, and this develops the brain. To dilute, adulterate, or even poison food and medicine for personal gain is not objectionable, since the destruction thereby of a few unwary consumers only proves their unfitness to survive in society. As in general commerce, so in private business, competition must be free. . . . All schemes of social reform are unscientific. Public charities tend to bolster up unworthy elements in society that nature has declared unfit to survive. Temperance reforms tend only to abridge individual liberty—for even the liberty to destroy one's self should be respected. Philanthropy is zeal without knowledge, while humanitarianism is fanaticism.

This general class of views antedated by many years the publication by Spencer and Darwin of their formulated doctrines of the "survival of the fittest" and "natural selection." But it cannot be denied that these doctrines, supported as they were by facts fresh from nature, have greatly strengthened this habit of thought. Nature's method is now much better known than formerly, and it is now well understood that an utterly soulless competition constitutes its fundamental characteristic. Surely man cannot go astray in following in the footsteps of nature. Let him learn from the animal world. He has descended from some of the humble stocks which he is now studying. Nature's plan has raised him from the condition of a beast to that of a rational being. It has created and developed society and civilisation. Unless tampered with by "reformers" all the operations of society would be competitive. Competition is the law of nature out of which progress results. Sociology, as its founder insisted, must be based on biology, and the true sociologist must understand this biologic law. Those who propose to apply methods to society which are opposed to the methods of nature are supposed to be ignorant of these fundamental truths and are called empiricists, "meddlers," and "tinkers."

Such, as I say, is the tenor and tendency of modern scientific thought. I do not say that all scientific men hold these views. I merely maintain that leading ones have formulated and inculcated them as natural deductions from the established facts of science, and that the public mind is rapidly assimilating them, while scarcely any attempts are being made to check their advance.

Is there any way of answering these arguments? Can the *laissez faire* doctrine be successfully met? . . . The present attempt to meet some parts of this argument is made in full consciousness of its strength as a factor in modern thought and with due deference to the great names that stand committed to it. The scientific facts which its defenders have brought to its support are, in the main, incontestable. To answer by denying these would be to abjure science and deserve contempt. The method of nature has been correctly interpreted. The doctrines of the survival of the fittest and natural selection are perfectly true doctrines. The law of competition is the fundamental law. It is unquestionably true that progress, not only in primary organic development, but also in society, has resulted from the action of this law.

After conceding all this, the attempt, notwithstanding, to stem the tide of modern scientific thought must, indeed, seem a hopeless one. At the outset it must be frankly acknowledged that if the current views are unsound the fault is not chargeable to science. If there is any defect it must lie in the inferences drawn from the facts and not in the facts themselves. . . .

In order to grapple at once with the whole problem let me answer these questions by the open charge that the modern scientific philosophers fail to recognise the true value of the *psychic factor*. Just as the metaphysicians lost their bearings by an empty worship of mind and made philosophy a plaything, so the modern evolutionists have missed their mark by degrading mind to a level with mechanical force. They seem thus about to fling away the grand results that the doctrine of evolution cannot otherwise fail to achieve. Far be it from me to appeal to the prejudices of the enemies of science by casting opprobrium upon scientific deductions, but when I consider the tendencies which are now so unmistakable, and which are so certainly the consequence of the protracted study, on the part of leading scientists, of the unquestionable methods of nature, I think I can, though holding precisely opposite opinions, fully sympathise with Carlyle in characterising the philosophy of evolution as a "gospel of dirt".... Let us approach the kernel of the problem.

The *laissez faire* doctrine fails to recognise that, in the development of mind, a virtually *new power* was introduced into the world.... Not to mention the great steps in the cosmical history of the solar system and of the earth, we must regard the evolution of protoplasm, the "physical basis of life," as one of those gigantic strides which thenceforth completely revolutionised the surface of our planet. The development of the cell as the unit of organisation was another such stride. The origin of vertebrate life introduced a new element, and the birth of man wrought still another transformation....

It is in this sense, and in this only, that I claim the development of mind—of the thinking, reasoning, inventing faculty of the human brain—as another, and one of the best marked, of the great cosmic strides that have characterised the course of evolution and belong to the legitimate methods of nature....

But all this may be regarded as mere generality. Let us come to something more specific. It has always been a marvel to my comprehension that wise men and philosophers, when smitten with the specious logic of the *laissez faire* school, can close their eyes to the most obtrusive fact that civilisation presents.... The great fact, then ... is that, in spite of all philosophy, whether mythologic, metaphysical, or naturalistic, declaring that man must and can do nothing, he *has*, from the very dawn of his intelligence, been transforming the entire surface of the planet he inhabits. No other animal performs anything comparable to what man performs. This is solely because no other possesses the developed psychic faculty.

If we analyse mind into its two departments, sense and intellect, we shall see that it is through this latter faculty that these results are accomplished. If we inquire more closely into the mode by which intellect operates, we shall find that it serves as a guiding power to those natural forces with which it is acquainted (and no others), directing them into channels of human advantage. If we seek for a single term by which to characterise with precision the nature of this process, we find this in *Invention*. The essential characteristic of all intellectual action is invention.

Glancing now at the *ensemble* of human achievement, which may be collectively called civilisation, we readily see that it is all the result of this inventive process. All practical art is merely the product of successful invention, and it requires no undue expansion of the term, nor extraordinary power of generalisation, to see in all human institutions only modified forms of arts, and true products of the intellectual, or inventive, faculty.

But what is the general result of all this? An entirely new dispensation has been given to the world. All the materials and forces of nature have been thus placed completely under the control of one of the otherwise least powerful of the creatures inhabiting the earth. He has only to know them in order to become their master. Nature has thus been made the servant of man. . . . When we confine our attention to the *élite* of mankind we do not need to have the ways specified in detail by which the powers of mind have exalted the intellectual being above all other products of creation. At the present moment the most dense and the most enlightened populations of the globe occupy what are termed temperate latitudes, which means latitudes in which for from three to five months each year vegetation ceases entirely, the waters are locked in ice, and the temperature frequently sinks far below the zero of the Fahrenheit thermometer. Imagine the thin-skinned, furless animal man subsisting in such a climate. Extinguish his fires, banish his clothing, blot out the habitations that deck the civilised landscape. How long would the puny race survive? But these are not products of nature, they are products of *art*, the wages of thought—fruits of the intellect.

When a well-clothed philosopher on a bitter winter's night sits in a warm room well lighted for his purpose and writes on a paper with pen and ink in the arbitrary characters of a highly developed language the statement that civilisation is the result of natural laws, and that man's duty is to let nature alone so that untrammeled it may work out a higher civilisation, he simply ignores every circumstance of his existence and deliberately closes his eyes to every fact within the range of his faculties. If man had acted upon his theory there would have been no civilisation, and our philosopher would have remained a troglodyte.*

But how shall we distinguish this human, or anthropic, method from the method of nature? Simply by reversing all the definitions. Art is the antithesis of nature. If we call one the natural method we must call the other the artificial method. If nature's process is rightly named natural selection, man's process is artificial selection. The survival of the fittest is simply the survival of the strong, which implies, and might as well be called, the destruction of the weak.

---

*[Editor's note: Troglodyte: literally, a cave-dweller.]

And if nature progresses through the destruction of the weak, man progresses through the *protection* of the weak. This is the essential distinction.

In human society the psychic power has operated to secure the protection of the weak in two distinct ways: first, by increasing the supply of the necessities of life, and, secondly by preventing the destruction of life through the enemies of man. The immediate instrumentality through which the first of these processes is carried on is art, the product of invention. The second process takes place through the establishment of positive institutions.

It is difficult to say which of these agencies has been most effective. Both were always indispensable, and therefore all comparison is unprofitable.

Art operates to protect the weak against adverse surroundings. It is directed against natural forces, chiefly physical. . . .

If, on the other hand, we inquire into the nature of human institutions, we shall perceive that they are of three kinds, tending to protect the weak in three ways, or ascending degrees. These three successively higher means through which this end is attained are, first, Justice, second, Morality, and third, Charity. These forms of action have been reached through the development, respectively, of the three corresponding sentiments: Equity, Beneficence, and Benevolence.

All of these altruistic sentiments are wholly unknown, or known only in the merest embryo, to all animals below man, and therefore no such means of protection exist among them. They are strictly human, or anthropic. Many evolutionists fail to recognise this. Some sociologists refuse to admit it. They look about and see so much injustice, immorality, and rapacity that they are led to suppose that only natural methods are in operation in society. This is a great mistake. In point of fact, the keener the sense of justice the more conspicuous the diminishing number of violations of it come to appear, and conversely, the obviousness of injustice proves the general prevalence of justice. It is the same with morality and philanthropy.

If we consider the effect of these three codes of human conduct in the direction of enabling the weaker ones to survive we shall see that it has been immense. Out of the first has arisen government, the chief value and function of which has always been and still is such protection. . . . No one could probably be found to gainsay that the moral law of society has exerted a salutary influence, yet its aim is strictly altruistic, opposed to the law of the survival of the fittest, and wholly in the direction of enabling those to survive who would not survive without its protection. Finally, the last sentiment to be developed, and doubtless the highest, is so universally recognised as peculiar to man that his very name has been given to it—the sentiment of *humanity.* ... It must be admitted that humanitarian institutions have done far less good than either juridical or ethical institutions. ... The institutions established to enforce it are for the most part poorly supported, badly managed, and often founded on a total misconception of human nature and of the true mode of attaining the end in view. ... But if ever humanitarian sentiments become diffused throughout the body politic, become the object of deep study, as have those of justice and right, it may be confidently predicted that society will prove itself capable of caring for the most unfortunate of its members in a manner that shall not work demoralisation.

In all these ways man, through his intelligence, has laboured successfully to resist the law of nature. His success is conclusively demonstrated by a comparison of his condition with that of other species of animals. No other cause can be assigned for his superiority. How can the naturalistic philosophers shut their eyes to such obvious facts? Yet, what is their attitude? They condemn all attempts to protect the weak, whether by private or public methods. They claim that it deteriorates the race by enabling the unfit to survive and transmit their inferiority. This is true only in certain cases of hereditary diseases or mental deficiencies, which should be taken account of by men because they are not by nature. Nothing is easier than to show that the unrestricted competition of nature does not secure the survival of the fittest possible, but only of the actually fittest, and in every attempt man makes to obtain something fitter than this actual fittest he succeeds, as witness improved breeds of animals and grafts of fruit. Now, the human method of protecting the weak deals in some such way with men. It not only increases the number but improves the quality.

But "government," at least, must *laisser faire.* It must not "meddle" with natural laws. The laws of trade, business, social intercourse, are natural laws, immutable and indestructible. All interference with them is vain. The fallacy here is a *non sequitur.* It may be readily granted that these laws are immutable and indestructible. Were this not the case it would certainly be hopeless to interfere with their action. But every mechanical invention proves that nothing is easier than to interfere successfully with the operation of these uniform natural forces. They have only to be first thoroughly understood and then they are easily *controlled*. To *destroy* a force is one thing, to control its action is quite another. Those who talk in this way involve themselves in the most palpable inconsistency. They must not be allowed to stop where they do. They must go on and carry their strictures to a logical conclusion. They must deny to government the right to protect its citizens from injustice. This is a clear interference with the natural laws of society. They must deny to society the right to enforce its code of morals. Nothing is more unnatural. They must suppress the healing art which keeps the sick from dying as they do among animals. Nor is this all. They must condemn all interference with physical laws and natural forces. To dam a stream must be characterised as a "vain" attempt to overcome a natural law. The wind must be left free to blow where it will, and not be forced against the fan of a wind-mill. The vapour of heated water must be allowed to float off naturally into the air and not be pent up in a steam-boiler and thence conducted into the cylinder of a steam-engine. All these things and every other device of inventive man are so many attempts to "violate" the laws of nature, which is declared impossible.

What then remains of the *laissez faire* doctrine? Nothing but this: That it is useless, and may be dangerous, to attempt to control natural forces until their character is first well understood. This is a proposition which is true for every department of force, and does not involve the surrender of the whole domain of sociology after it has been demonstrated that society is a theatre of forces.

The truth thus comes forth from a rational study of nature and human society that social progress has been due only in very slight degree to natural evolution as accomplished through the survival of the fittest, and its chief success has resulted from the reduction of competition in the struggle for existence and the protection of the weaker members. Such competition, in so far as it has been permitted to operate, has tended to lower the standard of the fittest and to check advancement. It is not, of course, claimed that the natural method has ever been fully overcome. It has always operated, and still operates, powerfully in many ways. It has been chiefly in the simpler departments of physical and mechanical phenomena that the psychic, or anthropic, method has superseded it. The inventive arts have been the result. Vital forces have yielded to some extent to the influence of mind in bringing about improved stocks of animals and vegetables, and even certain social laws have come under rational control through the establishment of institutions. Still, every step in this progress has been contested. It was not enough that the intellect was feeble and ill-fitted to grapple with such problems. It was not enough that ignorance of nature's laws should cause unnumbered failures. A still stronger barrier was presented by the intellect itself in the form of positive error embodied in philosophy. As already remarked, philosophy has always been negative and nihilistic, and has steadily antagonised the common sense of mankind. It is only quite recently that there has come into existence anything like a truly *positive* philosophy, *i.e.*, a philosophy of *action*. The intellectual power of enlightened man has at length become sufficient to grasp the problems of social life. A large body of truth has been accumulated by which to be guided in their solution. Positive error in the drawing of false conclusions from established facts is now the chief obstacle. Rational interpretation has come to prevail in all the lower departments of phenomena. It is chiefly in the complex departments of psychic and social action that error still holds sway. Nothing remains to be done but to apply the established canons of science to these higher fields of activity. Here there is still competition. Here the weaker still go to the wall. Here the strong are still the fittest to survive. Here Nature still practises her costly selection which always involves the destruction of the defenceless. The demand is for still further reduction of competition, still greater interference with the operations of natural forces, still more complete control of the laws of nature, and still more absolute supremacy of the psychic over the natural method of evolution.

These ends will be secured in proportion as the true nature of mind is understood. When nature comes to be regarded as passive and man as active, instead of the reverse as now, when human action is recognised as the most important of all forms of action, and when the power of the human intellect over vital, psychic and social phenomena is practically conceded, then, and then only, can man justly claim to have risen out of the animal and fully to have entered the human stage of development.

NATURAL LAW, ETHICS, AND EVOLUTION*

Josiah Royce

The discussion . . . seems to me to have reached a stage where it is just as well to supplement controversies over the precise meaning or

*From the *International Journal of Ethics*, 5 (1895), pp. 489–500.

the bearing of Professor Huxley's address, by a few independent efforts, however imperfect these may be, to deal with the questions: (1) whether the "ethical process" is a "part of the cosmical process"; and (2) whether it stands in a relation of opposition or of harmony to the tendencies of this cosmical process; and (3) finally, in case the relation of the "ethical process" to the "cosmical process" is one of opposition, what the source of this opposition is. . . .

The student of nature is trying to reduce observed facts to universal laws. In so far as he can do this, he succeeds in what certain recent students of the Logic of Science have called the description of the facts. The fundamental principle of empirical science is, that you can only tell what a given fact is, in so far as you can describe its nature in universal terms, *i.e.*, in terms which identify this nature with the nature of other facts. Were all the facts of our experience single, discontinuous, unrepeated even in memory, and as different from one another as tones are now different from odors, or as brightness is different from swiftness, then we might all of us experience the world; but we could none of us describe in the least what it contained. This world might even be allowed to have *one* sort of uniformity in it, it might be as richly delightful a world as you please, from moment to moment; but it would be not only an uncomprehended, but an unreported world, a world of whose facts no record could be made. On the other hand, a world where experience can be recorded, reported, described, has two characters: First, there are in it facts whose similarities can be noted, *i.e.*, there are "wholes" or "groups" of phenomenal elements, which are alike in some respects; and, secondly, the noted similarities are such as permit you, in terms of these similarities themselves, to define certain complex groups of phenomena, as "having the same structure," or as "being built up according to the same rule," or as "exemplifying the same law," so that at least some of the details of each fact noted are "explained" by this law. To "explain" a given phenomenal detail, noted in your experience, say d, by the "natural law" which is said to "require" its presence, or to "make it necessary," is simply to point out that the phenomenon d is part of a larger whole, a "fact" in the substantive sense, $abcd$, and that this "whole fact," $abcd$, has a structure, or "make-up," a describable "build," a "typical consti-tution," which other whole facts of experience, viz, ABCD, also exemplify, while this constitution is such as to involve the presence of d in case a, b, and c are present, and in case the whole is to preserve the aforesaid typical structure. You then say that, since the whole fact $abcd$ resembles ABCD, not in its details as such (*i.e.*, in its contents), but in their structural relations,—*i.e.*, in the general type or build of each of these whole facts,—therefore the same rule or law which defines D by its relations to the other phenomena, A,B,C, of its own group, . . . can be realized or exemplified when you pass to an *abc* group, only if there is present a fourth phenomenon, *d*, which is such as to have the same structural relation to *abc* in the whole fact whereof *abc* and *d* are parts, as was present in case of the facts ABCD.

My statement is abstract. But the principle is simple. It means that you cannot describe whole facts, that you cannot report, record, verify, or comprehend their structures, without conceiving the phenomenal details of these facts as subject to laws. . . . There is, indeed, no *a priori* principle that every experience which may occur to anybody is describable at all. Anybody's experience might be, to any extent, apparently or really unique. In so far as it was unique, science could only ignore it, as being a "private" or "personal" experience. . . .

Nature then, *in order to be describable*, has to be viewed or conceived as such that the details of every natural phenomenon shall be "subject to," "determined by," or "necessitated by," the laws which describe the structure of the phenomenal wholes of which each detail is a part. If any given natural phenomenon, itself a mere fragment (*e.g.*, the petal of a particular flower, the tooth of a carnivorous animal, the total phase of an individual lunar eclipse), is to be conceived as a part of a certain whole, then this part must be *conceived as if* "explained," or "necessitated," by the law which describes, in universal terms, the whole "thing" or "process" of which the fragment is a part. And this is what is meant by the "necessity" of natural events. Natural necessity is an incident of the conceived describability of natural phenomena when grouped in whole facts.

That natural phenomena shall be *conceived as* necessary, or as subject to rigid law, and that the "cosmic process" shall be viewed as one where "mere necessity reigns," is therefore not a belief capable of any but a relatively subjective and human interpretation. Experience comes and goes in its own way. No mortal has ever "experienced" the absolute necessity of any cosmic process whatever. Chance, as Mr. Charles S. Peirce has well observed, streams in through every channel of our senses. Trust then to mere experience, as it comes to any one of us, and such experience can never prove that there are "cosmic laws."

But natural science depends not upon merely accepting, but also upon reporting, and upon recording, the phenomena, upon comparing notes, upon trusting nobody's private experience as such, upon a process, then, of publicly verifiable description of facts. This process—not now the cosmic process, but the process of description—involves noting uniformities, and depends for its success upon our ability to note the latter. The describable uniformities are structural uniformities, *i.e.*, those expressible in terms of universal "rules of structure" or "laws." . . . The only further assumption upon which the doctrine of the *objective* universality of rigid cosmic laws, as distinct from the foregoing subjective and human need for such laws, depends, is the assumption . . . that, in our human experience, *only* the relatively describable data stand for the external or physical world *as such*, —the endless indescribabilities of our experience, the "chance" of Mr. Peirce's account, being viewed, by scientific thinking, as standing for the merely "individual" or "internal" element of our experience, or for the limitations of the individual point of view. For science . . . is an essentially social affair. The described "cosmical" fact is a fact which others are conceived to be capable of verifying besides the observer who now describes. And as only the describable aspect of our experience is communicable to others for them to verify, and as only the verifiable is, scientifically speaking, to be viewed as "cosmical" at all, it follows that, while private experience is full of what seems to be chance, we all have come to regard the cosmical process as one subject to the most rigid law. But one must carefully bear in mind this genesis and meaning of the whole concept, both of necessary natural law and of the cosmical processes themselves, in any comparison of the "cosmical process" with the "ethical process." . . .

On the other hand, the conception of moral laws, by which given acts are to be judged, and of "ethical processes," such as what is called "Progress"—processes which involve a gradual approach towards a conformity of given facts to given ethical ideals,—this whole conception of the moral world as such involves an entirely different point of view in the presence of human experience. To conceive the "cosmical process" as such, you have to conceive it as in every detail subject to . . . the cosmical laws. But you can well view the facts in the light of a moral ideal, while believing that the now existent physical facts run in some ways directly counter to the ideal. Yes, so to view the facts is inevitable whenever you have ideals. For you derive your ideals, ultimately, from an aspect of your experience which has not to do with describing experienced facts, but with desiring ideal objects that are absent when you desire them. It is true that what you rationally desire, you can in general both describe and hope ... to verify. ... But you do not desire the object *in so far as* it is describable. And furthermore, just in so far as you desire any object, its presence is not yet verifiable. One desires the absent. The cosmical fact, the physical fact, viewed as subject to natural law, is, then, an object in so far as it is *both* describable *and* verifiable. The object of our ideal is desirable *not* in so far as it is describable, and, again, *precisely in so far as it is not* yet verifiable. Herein, then, lies a double contrast between the natural fact as such, and the object of desire, as such. ... The future eclipse ... can be predicted as something necessary. ... The eclipse is also verifiable, at the time of its occurrence, by all rightly situated observers. But so far the eclipse is no object of desire. Desire is as vain as would be prayer. ...

In consequence, our present contrast might be stated thus: Phenomena are desired (or dreaded) precisely in so far as they appear to be *interestingly novel*. Novelty, then, is a *conditio sine qua non* of all ideal value when regarded from a temporal point of view. But phenomena are explicable precisely in so far as they are conceived as *not* novel, but as mere cases under law. And again: The desired, or the dreaded, must be, as such, *now* unverifiable. But the explained is known to be such precisely in so far as universal explanations are actually verified. ...

Here is the root of the endless conflict between the ethical view of the world and the explanatory or "scientific" view. For a rational ethical doctrine is simply some universalized system of desires. What the right system may be concerns us not here. Enough if one has an ideal, he bases it on some type of desire. If nothing were desirable, there would be no ideals. A man with an ethical doctrine has simply taught himself what he now thinks to be wisely desirable. But he still desires. Thus desiring, he looks out upon experience. There occur phenomena. These his science "apperceives," recognizes, describes as cases of law, explains, calls necessary. But the very nature of this explanatory or descriptive sort of consciousness is that it says, "these phenomena are not novel." The consciousness of the possessor of ideals, however, essentially asserts, at every breath one draws, "Yet the novel, in so far as it justly appears novel, is precisely what I want." The explaining consciousness insists: "The law is eternally realized. What has been will be. There seems to be alteration. There is none." The ethical consciousness retorts: "The law is not yet realized. In this 'not yet' is my life. I have no abiding city. I seek one out of sight." Meanwhile, of course, it is perfectly possible to point out common territory, where these two views seem to meet without direct conflict. "You must use my insight," says the explaining consciousness, "if you want to realize your ideals. In vain do you desire as ideal what my laws forbid as forever unverifiable." The ethical consciousness must accept this inevitable comment. But it still responds: "Whatever laws of yours I recognize, they become to me not my ideals, but the mere material for realizing my ideals. If I could not interfere with the phenomenal expression that your laws are to get, my work would be utterly vain. You point me the means. But I set the goal. I do not quarrel with your laws. But I use them."

Hereupon, of course, the explaining consciousness makes one retort which does, indeed, appear to be crushing. "Realize your ideals if you will and can," it says, "yet what is your realization but a mere incident of my cosmical process? Your realization, when it comes, will be a natural phenomenon, a part of a whole fact, like the rest. I shall explain this phenomenon, and show, whenever it happens, that it is nothing new." To this, of course, the ethical consciousness may make either one of two responses. It may say: "Granted. As a fact, I admit that you are right. My realization of my ideals will itself be only a nature-process, involving no true novelty. I admit that my view is, in the last analysis, illusory. 'Nature is made better by no mean, but nature makes that mean,' just as Mr. Herbert Spencer quotes. Nothing really new ever happens. Hence no ideals, viewed *as* ideals, ever do realize themselves, any more than eclipses come because we hope for them. But still our human experience has its limitations. Some events seem novel. Some desires seem, as such, productive of what nature did not before contain. As a fact, the 'star-mist' contained everything, —good, evil, possible, necessary. . . . Hence you have the truth; but I, as practical common sense, must live in my necessary illusions; and it is in *this* sense that I remain forever in opposition to you; just as an inevitable, if illusory, point of view."

This is what the ethical consciousness *may* say; and it is saying this which, to follow out to their just consequences the views of many writers, ought to constitute what such writers should consistently regard as the true "philosophy of evolution." The real world, thus viewed, is one of rigid cosmical law. In such a world, nothing essentially new ever happens. If we, as scientific observers, could come to comprehend this truth, we should no more talk of a genuine realization of ideals before unrealized in the universe, than we should regard the swing of a pendulum as a dramatic action. . . . New passions and desires, as well as their significant potency in transforming the world, are and must be illusions, if describable natural law, as such, is universal. . . . What has been will be. There is, then, nothing truly ethical. There is only the cosmical. This, I say, is the only possible "philosophy of evolution," if natural law is an account of the absolutely real world. Evolution, as a process, is in that case the mere appearance of novelties to unwary or to necessarily ignorant observers. It does not and cannot involve anything truly historical. But meanwhile, of course, the philosophical evolutionist of this type could make practical concessions, to his public, to himself, and to the ethical consciousness, so long as he did not forget that these concessions were such,—mere accommodations to human ignorance and to the practical point of view. He could say, "A portion of the cosmical process,—namely, our own voluntary activity, appears as if it were ethical, as if true novelty, genuine progress, effective ideals, historically significant passage to something never before realized, were there present." This illusion is human, inevitable, and even useful. When we write on ethics we have to treat this illusion as if it were true; and to do so is as harmless as to speak of the sunrise, remembering all the while the cosmical truth.

Such ethically disposed, but consistent, partisans of natural necessity ought, however, still to admit that the ethical process, when thus abstractly sundered from the cosmical process, of which it is all the while held to be a part, does indeed appear in very sharp contrast to the rest of the cosmical process. In the ethical world, illusory as it is here said to be, it still seems true that the pendulums do not merely swing, that the old does not merely recur, that the creation moves towards some far-off event, divine or diabolical. . . . One has to treat nature as if she could be made better. One looks to the future with hopes which, for many evolutionists, become rather sentimental. . . . But the abstraction is in sharp contrast to the supposed truth. The ethical world is, when conceived, in vehement, even if in illusory, opposition to the natural process; and Professor Huxley's discussion will have done great good, in so far as it leads to the recognition of this inevitable fact. How one states the details of the opposition is of small consequence. The opposition itself is deep and universal.

But the ethical consciousness might decline thus to abandon its assertions. It might say, "But, after all, my view is right. I not merely, in the seeming of my ideals, contrast my illusions with a supposed truth, but I rightly, and in the name of truth, oppose my view of the real world to any physical view. After all, does experience prove the real universality of the 'cosmical process'? Certainly, experience, as such, does not. That nothing new occurs is a proposition directly opposed to the seeming of every individual experience. Why may not this seeming be well founded? Why may there not be true novelties, effective ideals, genuine progress, transformations, evolution which is not a mere seeming of growth, spiritual processes which were not present in the star-mist in any form?" . . .

As a fact, the assertion of the universality of the rigid cosmical process . . . is unquestionably a human, and, as I myself should affirm, a distinctly social theory for the interpretation of one aspect of our experience. Take human experience from that special point of view, and *then*, indeed, you have to conceive the world of experience *as if it were known to be* one of cosmical processes, which are the same yesterday, to-day, and forever. In that world, the only philosophy of evolution is that all evolution is to be called appearance. The only ethical process observable is one which is to be received as unreal. There is no question of warring against the cosmical process. But there is question of an undying opposition between the inevitable but illusory ethical consciousness and the hypothetically true cosmical consciousness. . . .

But now, the other view of human experience, the one which regards the universe as what I have elsewhere called "The World of Appreciation," is, as a fact, equally true to experience, and equally inevitable. For nature we know, as a fact, only through our social consciousness, and the social consciousness is ethical before it is physical, appreciates more deeply than it describes, recognizes nature for reasons which are, in the last analysis, themselves ideal, and is conscious of novelty, of progress, of significance, in general of the human, in ways which, in the last analysis, make the whole cosmical process a mere appearance of one aspect of the moral world. Yet this doctrine is not "supernaturalism," because the true opponent of the natural is not the "supernatural," but the human. The "cosmos" in the sense of empirical science is a conceptual product of the human mind. Man is indeed but a fragment of the absolutely real universe. But that genuine universe of which he is a fragment is not the world of description, but the world of appreciation, — a world at which the phenomena of nature indeed richly hint, but which they do not reveal.

It is true that, when viewed in the light of such a doctrine, the facts of evolution get an interpretation, not here to be expounded, which does away with much of the opposition between the ethical and what had seemed the cosmical, in the sense in which we have so far used that word in this paper. . . . Meanwhile, I should still hold that, as points of view, the view for which the ethical process exists at all is very sharply opposed to the view which, in the sense of physical science, deals with cosmical processes as such. Call the whole matter one of phenomena and of human opinion, and then indeed this opposition need lead to no misunderstandings. It will then be *merely* one of many points of view, no assertions of ultimate truth being made on either side. But if it be a question of a philosophy of reality, then one must choose between the two points of view, or else reject both. There is no chance of reconciling the metaphysically real and ultimate universality of the so-called cosmical, *i.e.*, physical processes, or processes according to describably rigid laws, with any even remotely ethical interpretation of the same reality.

The questions asked at the outset are then to be decided thus: (1) Conceive the "cosmical process" as one of describably rigid law, as all explanation in natural science does, must do, and ought to do, and *then* the "ethical process" can form no part of the "cosmical process." (2) In essence the "ethical process," in so far as you conceive its presence at all, is utterly opposed to all "cosmical processes" when they are thus physically conceived. (3) The nature of the opposition lies not in any world of "things in themselves" at all, but in the peculiarity of the ethical point of view which, in dealing, as both this view and its rival concretely do, with mere human appearances, estimates ideally, and desires essential novelty, progress, and thus far unattained as such; while the descriptive or explanatory point of view conceives its purely phenomenal world as if it were known to contain no novelties whatever, and nothing ideal.

EVOLUTIONARY LOVE*

Charles Sanders Peirce

Philosophy, when just escaping from its golden pupa-skin, mythology, proclaimed the great evolutionary agency of the universe to be

*From *The Monist*, 3 (1893), pp. 176–200.

Love. Or, since this pirate-lingo, English, is poor in such-like words, let us say Eros, the exuberance-love. Afterwards, Empedocles* set up passionate-love and hate as the two coordinate powers of the universe. In some passages, kindness is the word. But certainly, in any sense in which it has an opposite, to be senior partner of that opposite, is the highest position that love can attain. Nevertheless, the ontological gospeller, in whose days those views were familiar topics, made the One Supreme Being, by whom all things have been made out of nothing, to be cherishing-love. What, then, can he say to hate? Never mind, at this time, what the scribe of the apocalypse, if he were John, stung at length by persecution into a rage unable to distinguish suggestions of evil from visions of heaven, and so become the Slanderer of God to men, may have dreamed. The question is rather what the sane John thought, or ought to have thought, in order to carry out his idea consistently. His statement that God is love seems aimed at that saying of Ecclesiastes that we cannot tell whether God bears us love or hatred. "Nay," says John, "we can tell, and very simply! We know and have trusted the love which God hath in us. God is love." There is no logic in this, unless it means that God loves all men. In the preceding paragraph, he had said, "God is light and in him is no darkness at all." We are to understand, then, that as darkness is merely the defect of light, so hatred and evil are mere imperfect stages of . . . love and loveliness. This concords with that utterance reported in John's Gospel: "God sent not the Son into the world to judge the world; but that the world should through him be saved. He that believeth on him is not judged: he that believeth not hath been judged already. . . . And this is the judgment, that the light is come into the world, and that men loved darkness rather than the light." That is to say, God visits no punishment on them; they punish themselves, by their natural affinity for the defective. Thus, the love that God is, is not a love of which hatred is the contrary; otherwise Satan would be a coordinate power; but it is a love which embraces hatred as an imperfect stage of it, an Anteros—yea, even needs hatred and hatefulness as its object. For self-love is no love; so if God's self is love, that which he loves must be defect of love; just as a luminary can light up only that which otherwise would be dark. . . .

The movement of love is circular, at one and the same impulse

---

*[Editor's note: Empedocles was a Greek philosopher of the fifth century, B.C.]

projecting creations into independency and drawing them into harmony. This seems complicated when stated so; but it is fully summed up in the simple formula we call the Golden Rule. This does not, of course, say, Do everything possible to gratify the egoistic impulses of others, but it says, Sacrifice your own perfection to the perfectionment of your neighbor. Nor must it for a moment be confounded with the Benthamite*... motto, Act for the greatest good of the greatest number. Love is not directed to abstractions but to persons; not to persons we do not know, nor to numbers of people, but to our own dear ones, our family and neighbors. "Our neighbor," we remember, is one whom we live near, not locally perhaps, but in life and feeling.

Everybody can see that the statement of St. John is the formula of an evolutionary philosophy, which teaches that growth comes only from love, from—I will not say self-*sacrifice*, but from the ardent impulse to fulfil another's highest impulse. Suppose, for example, that I have an idea that interests me. It is my creation. It is my creature.... I love it; and I will sink myself in perfecting it. It is not by dealing out cold justice to the circle of my ideas that I can make them grow, but by cherishing and tending them as I would the flowers in my garden. The philosophy we draw from John's gospel is that this is the way mind develops; and as for the cosmos, only so far as it yet is mind, and so has life, is it capable of further evolution. Love, recognising germs of loveliness in the hateful, gradually warms it into life, and makes it lovely....

The nineteenth century is now fast sinking into the grave, and we all begin to review its doings and to think what character it is destined to bear as compared with other centuries in the minds of future historians. It will be called, I guess, the Economical Century; for political economy has more direct relations with all the branches of its activity than has any other science. Well, political economy has its formula of redemption, too. It is this: Intelligence in the service of greed ensures the justest prices, the fairest contracts, the most enlightend conduct of all the dealings between men, and leads to the *summum bonum*, food in plenty and perfect comfort. Food

---

*[Editor's note: Jeremy Bentham (1748–1832) was an English reformer and philosopher who taught that public questions ought to be settled by a calculation of the greatest good for the greatest number.]

for whom? Why, for the greedy master of intelligence. I do not mean to say that this is one of the legitimate conclusions of political economy, the scientific character of which I fully acknowledge. But the study of doctrines, themselves true, will often temporarily encourage generalisations extremely false, as the study of physics has encouraged necessitarianism. What I say, then, is that the great attention paid to economical questions during our century has induced an exaggeration of the beneficial effects of greed and of the unfortunate results of sentiment, until there has resulted a philosophy which comes unwittingly to this, that greed is the great agent in the elevation of the human race and in the evolution of the universe.

I open a handbook of political economy,—the most typical and middling one I have at hand,—and there find some remarks of which I will here make a brief analysis. I omit qualifications, sops thrown to Cerberus, phrases to placate Christian prejudice, trappings which serve to hide from author and reader alike the ugly nakedness of the greed-god. But I have surveyed my position. The author enumerates "three motives to human action: the love of self; the love of a limited class having common interests and feelings with one's self; the love of mankind at large."

Remark, at the outset, what obsequious title is bestowed on greed,—"the love of self." Love! The second motive *is* love. In place of "a limited class" put "certain persons," and you have a fair description. Taking "class" in the old-fashioned sense, a weak kind of love is described. In the sequel, there seems to be some haziness as to the delimitation of this motive. By the love of mankind at large, the author does not mean that deep, subconscious passion that is properly so called; but merely public-spirit, perhaps little more than a fidget about pushing ideas. The author proceeds to a comparative estimate of the worth of these motives. Greed, says he, but using, of course, another word, "is not so great an evil as is commonly supposed. . . . Every man can promote his own interests a great deal more effectively than he can promote any one else's, or than any one else can promote his." Besides, as he remarks on another page, the more miserly a man is, the more good he does. The second motive "is the most dangerous one to which society is exposed." Love is all very pretty: "no higher or purer source of human happiness exists." (Ahem!) But it is a "source of enduring injury," and, in short, should be overruled by something wiser. What is this wiser motive? We shall see.

As for public spirit, it is rendered nugatory by the "difficulties in the way of its effective operation." For example, it might suggest putting checks upon the fecundity of the poor and the vicious; and "no measure of repression would be too severe," in the case of criminals. The hint is broad. But unfortunately, you cannot induce legislatures to take such measures, owing to the pestiferous "tender sentiments of man towards man." It thus appears, that public-spirit, or Benthamism, is not strong enough to be the effective tutor of love, (I am skipping to another page) which must therefore be handed over to "the motives which animate men in the pursuit of wealth," in which alone we can confide, and which "are in the highest degree beneficent." Yes, in the "highest degree" without exception are they beneficent to the being upon whom all their blessings are poured out, namely, the Self, whose "sole object," says the writer, in accumulating wealth is his individual "sustenance and enjoyment." Plainly, the author holds the notion that some other motive might be in a higher degree beneficent even for the man's self to be a paradox wanting in good sense. He seeks to glaze and modify his doctrine; but he lets the perspicacious reader see what his animating principle is; and when, holding the opinions I have repeated, he at the same time acknowledges that society could not exist upon a basis of intelligent greed alone, he simply pigeonholes himself as one of the eclectics of inharmonious opinions. He wants his mammon flavored with a *soupçon* of god.

The economists accuse those to whom the enunciation of their atrocious villainies communicates a thrill of horror of being *sentimentalists*. It may be so: I willingly confess to having some tincture of sentimentalism in me, God be thanked! Ever since the French Revolution brought this leaning of thought into ill-repute,—and not altogether undeservedly, I must admit, true, beautiful, and good as that great movement was,—it has been the tradition to picture sentimentalists as persons incapable of logical thought and unwilling to look facts in the eyes. This tradition may be classed with the French tradition that an Englishman says *godam* at every second sentence, the English tradition that an American talks about "Britishers," and the American tradition that a Frenchman carries forms of etiquette to an inconvenient extreme, in short with all those traditions which survive simply because the men who use their eyes and ears are few and far between. Doubtless some excuse there was for all those opinions in days gone by; and sentimentalism, when it was the fashionable amusement to spend one's evenings in a flood of tears over a woeful performance on a candle-litten stage, sometimes made itself a little ridiculous. But what after all is sentimentalism? It is an *ism*, a doctrine, namely, the doctrine that great respect should be paid to the natural judgments of the sensible heart. This is what sentimentalism precisely is; and I entreat the reader to consider whether to contemn it is not of all blasphemies the most degrading. Yet the nineteenth century has steadily condemned it, because it brought about the Reign of Terror. That it did so is true. Still, the whole question is one of *how much*. The reign of terror was very bad; but now the Gradgrind banner has been this century long flaunting in the face of heaven, with an insolence to provoke the very skies to scowl and rumble. Soon a flash and quick peal will shake economists quite out of their complacency, too late. The twentieth century, in its latter half, shall surely see the deluge-tempest burst upon the social order, — to clear upon a world as deep in ruin as that greed-philosophy has long plunged it into guilt. No post-thermidorian high jinks then!

So a miser is a beneficent power in a community, is he? With the same reason precisely, only in a much higher degree, you might pronounce the Wall Street sharp to be a good angel, who takes money from heedless persons not likely to guard it properly, who wrecks feeble enterprises better stopped, and who administers wholesome lessons to unwary scientific men, by passing worthless checks upon them, — as you did, the other day, to me, my millionaire Master in glomery, when you thought you saw your way to using my process without paying for it, and of so bequeathing to your children something to boast of their father about, — and who by a thousand wiles puts money at the service of intelligent greed, in his own person. Bernard Mandeville, in his "Fable of the Bees," maintains that private vices of all descriptions are public benefits, and proves it, too, quite as cogently as the economist proves his point concerning the miser. He even argues, with no slight force, that but for vice civilisation would never have existed. In the same spirit, it has been strongly maintained and is to-day widely believed that all acts of charity and benevolence, private and public, go seriously to degrade the human race.

The "Origin of Species" of Darwin merely extends politico-economical views of progress to the entire realm of animal and vegetable life. The vast majority of our contemporary naturalists hold the opinion that the true cause of those exquisite and marvellous adaptations of nature for which, when I was a boy, men used to extol the divine wisdom is that creatures are so crowded together that those of them that happen to have the slightest advantage force those less pushing into situations unfavorable to multiplication or even kill them before they reach the age of reproduction. Among animals, the mere mechanical individualism is vastly reenforced as a power making for good by the animal's ruthless greed. As Darwin puts it on his title-page, it is the struggle for existence; and he should have added for his motto: Every individual for himself, and the Devil take the hindmost! Jesus, in his sermon on the Mount, expressed a different opinion.

Here, then, is the issue. The gospel of Christ says that progress comes from every individual merging his individuality in sympathy with his neighbors. On the other side, the conviction of the nine-teenth century is that progress takes place by virtue of every individual's striving for himself with all his might and trampling his neighbor under foot whenever he gets a chance to do so. This may accurately be called the Gospel of Greed. . . .

Natural selection, as conceived by Darwin, is a mode of evolu-tion in which the only positive agent of change in the whole passage from moner to man is fortuitous variation. To secure advance in a definite direction chance has to be seconded by some action that shall hinder the propagation of some varieties or stimulate that of others. In natural selection, strictly so called, it is the crowding out of the weak. . . .

The "Origin of the Species" was published toward the end of the year 1859. The preceding years . . . had been one of the most productive seasons,—or if extended so as to cover the great book we are considering, *the* most productive period of equal length in the entire history of science from its beginnings until now. The idea that chance begets order, which is one of the corner-stones of modern physics . . . was at that time put into its clearest light. . . . The consequence was that the idea that fortuitous events may result in a physical law . . . had taken a strong hold upon the minds of all who were abreast of the leaders of thought. By such minds, it was inevitable that the "Origin of Species," whose teaching was simply the application of the same principle to . . . organic development, should be hailed and welcomed. . . . Mechanism was now known to be all, or very nearly so. All this time, utilitarianism,—that improved substitute for the Gospel,—was in its fullest feather; and was a natural ally of an individualistic theory. . . . Another thing: anæs-thetics had been in use for thirteen years. Already, people's acquaint-ance with suffering had dropped off very much; and as a consequence, that unlovely hardness by which our times are so contrasted with those that immediately preceded them, had already set in, and inclined people to relish a ruthless theory. The reader would quite mistake the drift of what I am saying if he were to understand me as wishing to suggest that any of those things ... influenced Darwin himself. What I mean is that his hypothesis, while without dispute one of the most ingenious and pretty ever devised, and while argued with a wealth of knowledge, a strength of logic, a charm of rhetoric, and above all with a certain magnetic genuineness that was almost irresistible, did not appear, at first, at all near to being proved; and to a sober mind its case looks less hopeful now than it did twenty years ago; but the extraordinarily favorable reception it met with was plainly owing, in large measure, to its ideas being those toward which the age was favorably disposed, especially, because of the encouragement it gave to the greed-philosophy.

CHAPTER 4

Darwinism as
a Way of Thinking

INTRODUCTION

During the nineteenth century, most of the intellectuals who concerned themselves with Darwinism concentrated their attention on its substantive findings and its seeming implications for religion or social ethics. The things that caught the eyes of men like Asa Gray or John Fiske were the kinds of conclusions about the world that Darwin's premises seemed to point toward. But in the long run, Darwinism's most lasting intellectual significance lay not in its findings, or even in their possible implications, but in the new intellectual procedures or methods it appeared to introduce. In the social sciences, for example, the question of whether the natural sciences justified cooperative or competitive societies eventually gave way to methodological questions like: how can social institutions be studied in such a way as to bring to light their adaptive functions? In philosophy, debates on whether the universe at large was ruled by love or strife were gradually dropped in favor of such questions as: how can people best investigate a world in which no categories and no general facts are fixed and final?

Thorstein Veblen (1875–1929) and John Dewey (1859–1952) faced the methodological issue directly and brilliantly in two of the finest pieces of writing prompted by the *Origin:* Veblen's "Why Is Economics Not an Evolutionary Science?" (1898), and Dewey's "The Influence of Darwinism on Philosophy" (1909), both of which appear in this chapter. For Veblen and Dewey, the real import of Darwinism was not that it challenged the conclusions of older systems of economics or philosophy, but that it undermined all pre-Darwinian modes of inquiry. Conversely, Darwinism did not seem to either Veblen or Dewey to point so much toward specific new findings as toward new ways of thinking, toward a new logic of nature, man, and society.

METHODOLOGICAL-   STRIFE - CONFLICT.

MULLED - PONDER.   EMANCIPATE - SET FREE.

In different ways, Dewey and Veblen were both active reformers, not just of their academic disciplines—Dewey's psychology and philosophy, Veblen's economics and social anthropology—but of institutions. After older men had for half a century mulled over the meaning of Darwinism, Dewey and Veblen seized on what they thought was the inner secret of the *Origin* and used it as a weapon of liberation from the confines of what they both called "classical" ways of thinking. They were very self-consciously trying to identify themselves as members of a new and intellectually emancipated generation, a generation that believed it was no longer subject to worn conceptual formulas or inherited social arrangements. In their desire to be free, they invested Darwinism with meanings that neither Darwin himself nor the first generation of his readers would have recognized. Thus their essays, like the writings of many of their contemporaries during the Progressive years, have a quality of exaggerated confidence that new techniques of inquiry could reshape both the world of the mind and the other, more stubborn world of social realities.

For all the cocky exuberance with which Dewey and Veblen felt that they were members of the first really modern generation, the lesson they derived from Darwinism was one of what Veblen himself might have called "conspicuous humility." For centuries, philosophy and science had dealt in things "ceremonial" and "sacred," they thought, claiming to be sources of cosmic "laws" of one sort or another. During most of the nineteenth century, the very function of thought had been presumed to be the discovery of binding models of behavior, whether the discoveries came through theology, science, or philosophical theorizing about ways so-called normal men and societies ought to behave. Here, for both Veblen and Dewey, was the nub of what they meant by "classical." Being modern, then, meant giving up such dreams and adopting programs of inquiry that would be matter-of-fact and workable. The outcome of this combination of cocksureness and modesty, not only in Dewey and Veblen but in many of their contemporaries, was the creation of an intellectual style that is clearly recognizable as a prominent feature of the culture of intellectuals in the first half of the twentieth century. This style admitted that transcendentally grand questions have no secure answers, but insisted that there are other questions, more present and pressing, which the human mind may with luck and cunning be able to subdue.

CONSPICUOUS- VERY NOTICEABLE.

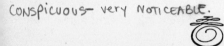

Adept - highly skilled.

WHY IS ECONOMICS NOT
AN EVOLUTIONARY SCIENCE?*

Thorstein Veblen

It may be taken as the consensus of those men who are doing the serious work of modern anthropology, ethnology, and psychology, as well as of those in the biological sciences proper, that economics is helplessly behind the times, and unable to handle its subject-matter in a way to entitle it to standing as a modern science. . . . The men of the sciences that are proud to own themselves "modern" find fault with the economists for being still content to occupy themselves with repairing a structure and doctrines and maxims resting on natural rights, utilitarianism, and administrative expediency. . . . These modern sciences are evolutionary sciences, and their adepts contemplate that characteristic of their work with some complacency. Economics is not an evolutionary science—by the confession of its spokesmen; and the economists turn their eyes with something of envy and some sense of baffled emulation to these rivals that make broad their phylacteries with the legend, "Up to date."

Precisely wherein the social and political sciences, including economics, fall short of being evolutionary sciences, is not so plain. At least, it has not been satisfactorily pointed out by their critics. Their successful rivals in this matter—the sciences that deal with human nature among the rest—claim as their substantial distinction that they are realistic; they deal with facts. But economics, too, is realistic in this sense: it deals with facts, often in the most painstaking way. . . . Any evolutionary science, on the other hand, is a close-knit body of theory. It is a theory of a process, of an unfolding sequence. But here, again, economics seems to meet the test in a fair measure, without satisfying its critics that its credentials are good. . . .

The difference between the evolutionary and the pre-evolutionary sciences lies not in the insistence on facts. . . . Nor does the difference lie in the absence of efforts to formulate and explain schemes of process, sequence, growth, and development. . . . The difference is a difference of spiritual attitude or point of view in the two contrasted generations of scientists. . . . With the earlier as with the later generation the basis of valuation of the facts handled is, in matters of detail, the causal relation which is apprehended to sub-

EMULATION- TRY TO EQUAL OR EXCEL.

*From the *Quarterly Journal of Economics*, 12 (1898), pp. 373–97.

DESERTS – ONE WHO DESERVES.
PROPENSITY – PARTICULAR INTEREST OR INCLINATION.

sist between them. . . . But in their handling of the more comprehensive schemes of sequence and relation . . . the two generations differ. The modern scientist is unwilling to depart from the test of causal relation or quantitative sequence. When he asks the question, Why? he insists on an answer in terms of cause and effect. He wants to reduce his solution of all problems to terms of the conservation of energy or the persistence of quantity. This is his last recourse. And this last recourse has in our time been made available for the handling of schemes of development and theories of a comprehensive process by the notion of a cumulative causation. The great deserts of the evolutionist leaders—if they have great deserts as leaders—lie, on the one hand, in their refusal to go back to the colorless sequence of phenomena and seek higher ground for their ultimate syntheses, and, on the other hand, in their having shown how this colorless impersonal sequence of cause and effect can be made use of for theory proper, by virtue of its cumulative character.

For the earlier natural scientists, as for the classical economists, this ground of cause and effect is not definitive. Their sense of truth and substantiality is not satisfied with a formulation of mechanical sequence. The ultimate term in their systematisation of knowledge is a "natural law." This natural law is felt to exercise some sort of a coercive surveillance over the sequence of events, and to give a spiritual stability and consistence to the causal relation at any given juncture. To meet the high classical requirement, a sequence—and a developmental process especially—must be apprehended in terms of a consistent propensity tending to some spiritually legitimate end. . . . The objective point of the efforts of the scientists working under the guidance of this classical tradition, is to formulate knowledge in terms of absolute truth; and this absolute truth is a spiritual fact. It means a coincidence of facts with the deliverances of an enlightened and deliberate common sense.

The development . . . of this preconception of normality or of a propensity in events might be traced in detail from primitive animism down through the elaborate discipline of faith and metaphysics, overruling Providence, order of nature, natural rights, natural law, underlying principles. But all that may be necessary here is to point out that, by descent and by psychological content, this constraining normality is of a spiritual kind. It is for the scientific purpose an imputation of spiritual coherence to the facts dealt with. The question of interest is how this preconception of normality has fared at the hands of modern science, and how it has come to be superseded in the intellectual primacy by the latter-day preconception of a non-spiritual sequence. This question is of interest because its answer may throw light on the question as to what chance there is for the indefinite persistence of this archaic habit of thought in the methods of economic science. . . .

The standpoint of the classical economists, in their higher or definitive syntheses and generalisations, may not inaptly be called the standpoint of ceremonial adequacy. The ultimate laws and principles which they formulated were laws of the normal or the natural, according to a preconception regarding the ends to which, in the nature of things, all things tend. In effect, this preconception imputes to things a tendency to work out what the instructed common sense of the time accepts as the adequate or worthy end of human effort. It is a projection of the accepted ideal of conduct. This ideal of conduct is made to serve as a canon of truth, to the extent that the investigator contents himself with an appeal to its legitimation for premises that run back of the facts with which he is immediately dealing, for the "controlling principles" that are conceived intangibly to underlie the process discussed, and for the "tendencies" that run beyond the situation as it lies before him. . . . Features of the process that do not lend themselves to interpretation in the terms of the formula are abnormal cases and are due to disturbing causes. In all this the agencies or forces causally at work in the economic life process are neatly avoided. The outcome of the method, at its best, is a body of logically consistent propositions concerning the normal relation of things—a system of economic taxonomy. At its worst, it is a body of maxims for the conduct of business and a polemical discussion of disputed points of policy.

In all this, economic science is living over again in its turn the experiences which the natural sciences passed through some time back. In the natural sciences the work of the taxonomist was and continues to be of great value, but the scientists grew restless under the régime of symmetry and system-making. They took to asking why, and so shifted their inquiries from the structure of the coral reefs to the structure and habits of life of the polyp that lives in and by them. In the science of plants, systematic botany has not ceased to be of service; but the stress of investigation and discussion among the botanists to-day falls on the biological value of any given feature of structure, function, or tissue rather than on its taxonomic bearing. . . . The inquiry now looks consistently to the life process, and aims to explain it in terms of cumulative causation. . . .

But what does all this signify? . . . What are we going to do about it? The question is rather, What are we doing about it? There is the economic life process still in great measure awaiting theoretical formulation. The active material in which the economic process goes on is the human material of the industrial community. For the purpose of economic science the process of cumulative change that is to be accounted for is the sequence of change in the methods of doing things,—the methods of dealing with the material means of life.

What has been done in the way of inquiry into this economic life process? The ways and means of turning material objects and circumstances to account lie before the investigator at any given point of time in the form of mechanical contrivances and arrangements for compassing certain mechanical ends. It has therefore been easy to accept these ways and means as items of inert matter having a given mechanical structure and thereby serving the material ends of man. As such, they have been scheduled and graded by the economists under the head of capital, this capital being conceived as a mass of material objects serviceable for human use. This is well enough for the purposes of taxonomy; but it is not an effective method of conceiving the matter for the purpose of a theory of the developmental process. For the latter purpose, when taken as items in the process of cumulative change or as items in the scheme of life, these productive goods are facts of human knowledge, skill, and predilection; that is to say, they are, substantially, prevalent habits of thought, and it is as such that they enter into the process of industrial development. The physical properties of the materials accessible to man are constants: it is the human agent that changes, —his insight and his appreciation of what these things can be used for is what develops. The accumulation of goods already on hand conditions his handling and utilisation of the materials offered, but even on this side—the "limitation of industry by capital"—the limitation imposed is on what men can do and on the methods of doing it. The changes that take place in the mechanical contrivances are an expression of changes in the human factor. Changes in the material facts breed further change only through the human factor. It is in the human material that the continuity of development is to be looked for; and it is here, therefore, that the motor forces of the process of economic development must be studied if they are to be studied in action at all. Economic action must be the subject-matter of the science if the science is to fall into line as an evolutionary science. . . .

In all the received formulations of economic theory . . . the human material with which the inquiry is concerned is conceived in hedonistic terms; that is to say, in terms of a passive and substantially inert and immutably given human nature. The psychological and anthropological preconceptions of the economists have been those which were accepted by the psychological and social sciences some generations ago. The hedonistic conception of man is that of a lightning calculator of pleasures and pains, who oscillates like a homogeneous globule of desire of happiness under the impulse of stimuli that shift him about the area, but leave him intact. He has neither antecedent nor consequent. He is an isolated, definitive human datum, in stable equilibrium except for the buffets of the impinging forces that displace him in one direction or another. Self-imposed in elemental space, he spins symmetrically about his own spiritual axis until the parallelogram of forces bears down upon him, whereupon he follows the line of the resultant. When the force of the impact is spent, he comes to rest, a self-contained globule of desire as before. Spiritually, the hedonistic man is not a prime mover. He is not the seat of a process of living, except in the sense that he is subject to a series of permutations enforced upon him by circumstances external and alien to him.

The later psychology, reenforced by modern anthropological research, gives a different conception of human nature. According to this conception, it is the characteristic of man to do something, not simply to suffer pleasures and pains through the impact of suitable forces. He is not simply a bundle of desires that are to be saturated by being placed in the path of the forces of the environment, but rather a coherent structure of propensities and habits which seeks realisation and expression in an unfolding activity. According to this view, human activity, and economic activity among the rest, is not apprehended as something incidental to the process of saturating given desires. The activity is itself the substantial fact of the process, and the desires under whose guidance the action takes place are circumstances of temperament which determine the specific direction in which the activity will unfold itself in the given case. These circumstances of temperament are ultimate and definitive for the individual who acts under them, so far as regards his attitude as agent in the particular action in which he is engaged. But, in view of the science, they are elements of the existing frame of mind of the agent, and are the outcome of his antecedents and his life up to the point at which he stands. They are the products of his hereditary traits and his past experience, cumulatively wrought out under a given body of traditions, conventionalities, and material circumstances; and they afford the point of departure for the next step in the process. The economic life history of the individual is a cumulative process of adaptation of means to ends that cumulatively change as the process goes on, both the agent and his environment being at any point the outcome of the last process. His methods of life to-day are enforced upon him by his habits of life carried over from yesterday and by the circumstances left as the mechanical residue of the life of yesterday.

What is true of the individual in this respect is true of the group in which he lives. All economic change is a change in the economic community,—a change in the community's methods of turning material things to account. The change is always in the last resort a change in habits of thought. This is true even of changes in the mechanical processes of industry. A given contrivance for effecting certain material ends becomes a circumstance which affects the further growth of habits of thought—habitual methods of procedure—and so becomes a point of departure for further development of the methods of compassing the ends sought and for the further variation of ends that are sought to be compassed. In all this flux there is no definitively adequate method of life and no definitive or absolutely worthy end of action, so far as concerns the science which sets out to formulate a theory of the process of economic life. What remains as a hard and fast residue is the fact of activity directed to an objective end. Economic action is teleological, in the sense that men always and everywhere seek to do something. What, in specific detail, they seek, is not to be answered except by a scrutiny of the details of their activity; but, so long as we have to do with their life as members of the economic community, there remains the generic fact that their life is an unfolding activity of a teleological kind. . . .

The economic life history of any community is its life history in so far as it is shaped by men's interest in the material means of life. This economic interest has counted for much in shaping the cultural growth of all communities. Primarily and most obviously, it has guided the formation, the cumulative growth, of that range of conventionalities and methods of life that are currently recognized as economic institutions; but the same interest has also pervaded the community's life and its cultural growth at points where the resulting structural features are not chiefly and most immediately of an economic bearing. The economic interest goes with men through life, and it goes with the race throughout its process of cultural development. It affects the cultural structure at all points, so that all institutions may be said to be in some measure economic institutions. This is necessarily the case, since the base of action—the point of departure—in any step in the process is the entire organic complex of habits of thought that have been shaped by the past process. The economic interest does not act in isolation, for it is but one of several vaguely isolable interests on which the complex of teleological activity carried out by the individual proceeds. The individual is but a single agent in each case; and he enters into each successive action as a whole, although the specific end sought in a given action may be sought avowedly on the basis of a particular interest; as e.g., the economic, aesthetic, sexual, humanitarian, devotional interests. Since each of these passably isolable interests is a propensity of the organic agent man, with his complex of habits of thought, the expression of each is affected by habits of life formed under the guidance of all the rest. There is, therefore, no neatly isolable range of cultural phenomena that can be rigorously set apart under the head of economic institutions, although a category of "economic institutions" may be of service as a convenient caption, comprising those institutions in which the economic interest more immediately and consistently finds expression, and which most immediately and with the least limitation are of an economic bearing.

From what has been said it appears that an evolutionary economics must be the theory of a process of cultural growth as determined by the economic interest, a theory of a cumulative sequence of economic institutions stated in terms of the process itself. . . .

We are now ready to return to the question why economics is not an evolutionary science. It is necessarily the aim of such an economics to trace the cumulative working-out of the economic interest in the cultural sequence. It must be a theory of the economic life process of the race or the community. The economists have accepted the hedonistic preconceptions concerning human nature and human action, and the conception of the economic interest which a hedonistic psychology gives does not afford material for a theory of the development of human nature. Under hedonism the economic interest is not conceived in terms of action. It is therefore not readily apprehended or appreciated in terms of a cumulative growth of habits of thought, and does not provoke, even if it did lend itself to, treatment by the evolutionary method. . . . The premises and the point of view required for an evolutionary economics have been wanting. . . . The well-worn paths are easy to follow and lead into good company. . . . It is only when the methods of the science and the syntheses resulting from their use come to be out of line with habits of thought that prevail in other matters that the scientist grows restive under the guidance of the received methods and standpoints, and seeks a way out. Like other men, the economist is an individual with but one intelligence. He is a creature of habits and propensities given through the antecedents, heredity and cultural, of which he is an outcome; and the habits of thought formed in any one line of experience affect his thinking in any other. Methods of observation and of handling facts that are familiar through habitual use in the general range of knowledge, gradually assert themselves in any given special range of knowledge. They may be accepted slowly and with reluctance where their acceptance involves innovation; but if they have the continued backing of the general body of experience, it is only a question of time when they shall come into dominance in the special field. . . .

In the general body of knowledge in modern times the facts are apprehended in terms of causal sequence. This is especially true of that knowledge of brute facts which is shaped by the exigencies of the modern mechanical industry. To men thoroughly imbued with this matter-of-fact habit of mind the laws and theorems of economics, and of the other sciences that treat of the normal course of things, have a character of "unreality" and futility that bars out any serious interest in their discussion. The laws and theorems are "unreal" to them because they are not to be apprehended in the terms which these men make use of in handling the facts with which they are perforce habitually occupied. The same matter-of-fact spiritual attitude and mode of procedure have now made their way well up into the higher levels of scientific knowledge, even in the sciences which deal in a more elementary way with the same human material that makes the subject-matter of economics, and the economists themselves are beginning to feel the unreality of their theorems about "normal" cases. Provided the practical exigencies of modern industrial life continue of the same character as they now are, and so continue to enforce the impersonal method of knowledge, it is only a question of time when that (substantially animistic) habit of mind which proceeds on the notion of a definitive normality shall be displaced in the field of economic inquiry by that (substantially materialistic) habit of mind which seeks a comprehension of facts in terms of a cumulative sequence.

The later method of apprehending and assimilating facts and handling them for the purposes of knowledge may be better or worse, more or less worthy or adequate, than the earlier; it may be of greater or less ceremonial or aesthetic effect; we may be moved to regret the incursion of underbred habits of thought into the scholar's domain. But all that is beside the present point. Under the stress of modern technological exigencies, men's everyday habits of thought are falling into the lines that in the sciences constitute the evolutionary method; and knowledge which proceeds on a higher, more archaic plane is becoming alien and meaningless to them. The social and political sciences must follow the drift, for they are already caught in it.

THE INFLUENCE OF DARWINISM ON PHILOSOPHY*

John Dewey

That the publication of the *Origin of Species* marked an epoch in the development of the natural sciences is well known to the layman. That the combination of the very words origin and species embodied an intellectual revolt and introduced a new intellectual temper is easily overlooked by the expert. The conceptions that had reigned in the philosophy of nature and knowledge for two thousand years, the conceptions that had become the familiar furniture of the mind, rested on the assumption of the superiority of the fixed and final; they rested upon treating change and origin as signs of defect and unreality. In laying hands upon the sacred ark of absolute permanency, in treating the forms that had been regarded as types of fixity and perfection as originating and passing away, the *Origin of Species* introduced a mode of thinking that in the end was bound to transform the logic of knowledge, and hence the treatment of morals, politics, and religion.

No wonder, then, that the publication of Darwin's book, a half century ago, precipitated a crisis. The true nature of the controversy is easily concealed from us, however, by the theological clamor that attended it. The vivid and popular features of the anti-Darwinian row tended to leave the impression that the issue was between science on one side and theology on the other. Such was not the case—the issue lay primarily within science itself, as Darwin himself early recognized. The theological outcry he discounted from the start, hardly noticing it save as it bore upon the

---

*From Dewey, *The Influence of Darwinism on Philosophy and Other Essays in Contemporary Thought* (New York: Henry Holt & Co., 1910), pp. 1–19.

"feelings of his female relatives." But for two decades before final publication he contemplated the possibility of being put down by his scientific peers as a fool or as crazy. . . .

Religious considerations lent fervor to the controversy, but they did not provoke it. Intellectually, religious emotions are not creative but conservative. They attach themselves readily to the current view of the world and consecrate it. They steep and dye intellectual fabrics in the seething vat of emotions; they do not form their warp and woof. There is not, I think, an instance of any large idea about the world being independently generated by religion. Although the ideas that rose up like armed men against Darwinism owed their intensity to religious associations, their origin and meaning are to be sought in science and philosophy, not in religion.

Few words in our language foreshorten intellectual history as much as does the word species. The Greeks, in initiating the intellectual life of Europe, were impressed by characteristic traits of the life of plants and animals; so impressed indeed that they made these traits the key to defining nature and to explaining mind and society. And truly, life is so wonderful that a seemingly successful reading of its mystery might well lead men to believe that the key to the secrets of heaven and earth was in their hands. The Greek rendering of this mystery, the Greek formulation of the aim and standard of knowledge, was in the course of time embodied in the word species, and it controlled philosophy for two thousand years. To understand the intellectual face-about expressed in the phrase "origin of species," we must, then, understand the long dominant idea against which it is a protest.

Consider how men were impressed by the facts of life. Their eyes fell upon certain things slight in bulk, and frail in structure. To every appearance, these perceived things were inert and passive. Suddenly, under certain circumstances, these things—henceforth known as seeds or eggs or germs—begin to change, to change rapidly in size, form, and qualities. Rapid and extensive changes occur, however, in many things—as when wood is touched by fire. But the changes in the living thing are orderly; they are cumulative; they tend constantly in one direction; they do not, like other changes, destroy or consume, or pass fruitless into wandering flux; they realize and fulfil. Each successive stage, no matter how unlike its predecessor, preserves its net effect and also prepares the way for a fuller activity on the part of its successor. In living beings, changes do not happen as they seem to happen elsewhere, any which way; the earlier changes are regulated in view of later results. This progressive organization does not cease till there is achieved a true final term, a completed, perfected end. This final form exercises in turn a plenitude of functions, not the least noteworthy of which is production of germs like those from which it took its own origin, germs capable of the same cycle of self-fulfilling activity.

But the whole miraculous tale is not yet told. The same drama is enacted to the same destiny in countless myriads of individuals so sundered in time, so severed in space, that they have no opportunity for mutual consultation and no means of interaction. As an old writer quaintly said, "Things of the same kind go through the same formalities"—celebrate, as it were, the same ceremonial rites.

This formal activity which operates throughout a series of changes and holds them to a single course; which subordinates their aimless flux to its own perfect manifestation; which, leaping the boundaries of space and time, keeps individuals distant in space and remote in time to a uniform type of structure and function: this principle seemed to give insight into the very nature of reality itself. To it Aristotle gave the name . . . the scholastics translated as *species*.

The force of this term was deepened by its application to everything in the universe that observes order in flux and manifests constancy through change. From the casual drift of daily weather, through the uneven recurrence of seasons and unequal return of seed time and harvest, up to the majestic sweep of the heavens—the image of eternity in time—and from this to the unchanging pure and contemplative intelligence beyond nature lies one unbroken fulfilment of ends. Nature as a whole is a progressive realization of purpose strictly comparable to the realization of purpose in any single plant or animal.

The conception of species, a fixed form and final cause, was the central principle of knowledge as well as of nature. Upon it rested the logic of science. Change as change is mere flux and lapse; it insults intelligence. Genuinely to know is to grasp a permanent end that realizes itself through changes, holding them thereby within the metes and bounds of fixed truth. Completely to know is to relate all special forms to their one single end and good: pure contemplative intelligence. Since, however, the scene of nature which directly confronts us is in change, nature as directly and practically experienced does not satisfy the conditions of knowledge. Human experience is in flux, and hence the instrumentalities of sense-perception and of inference based upon observation are condemned in advance. Science is compelled to aim at realities lying behind and beyond the processes of nature, and to carry on its search for these realities by means of rational forms transcending ordinary modes of perception and inference.

There are, indeed, but two alternative courses. We must either find the appropriate objects and organs of knowledge in the mutual interactions of changing things; or else, to escape the infection of change, we *must* seek them in some transcendent and supernal region. The human mind, deliberately as it were, exhausted the logic of the changeless, the final, and the transcendent, before it essayed adventure on the pathless wastes of generation and transformation. . . .

Darwin was not, of course, the first to question the classic philosophy of nature and of knowledge. . . . Without the methods of Copernicus, Kepler, Galileo, and their successors in astronomy, physics, and chemistry, Darwin would have been helpless in the organic sciences. But prior to Darwin the impact of the new scientific method upon life, mind, and politics, had been arrested, because between these ideal or moral interests and the inorganic world intervened the kingdom of plants and animals. The gates of the garden of life were barred to the new ideas; and only through this garden was there access to mind and politics. The influence of Darwin upon philosophy resides in his having conquered the phenomena of life for the principle of transition, and thereby freed the new logic for application to mind and morals and life. . . .

The exact bearings upon philosophy of the new logical outlook are, of course, as yet, uncertain and inchoate. We live in the twilight of intellectual transition. One must add the rashness of the prophet to the stubbornness of the partisan to venture a systematic exposition of the influence upon philosophy of the Darwinian method. At best, we can but inquire as to its general bearing—the effect upon mental temper and complexion, upon that body of half-conscious, half-instinctive intellectual aversions and preferences which determine, after all, our more deliberate intellectual enterprises. In this vague inquiry there happens to exist as a kind of touchstone a problem of long historic currency that has also been much discussed in Darwinian literature. I refer to the old problem of design *versus* chance, mind *versus* matter, as the causal explanation, first or final, of things.

As we have already seen, the classic notion of species carried with it the idea of purpose. In all living forms, a specific type is present directing the earlier stages of growth to the realization of its own perfection. Since this purposive regulative principle is not visible to the senses, it follows that it must be an ideal or rational force. Since, however, the perfect form is gradually approximated through the sensible changes, it also follows that in and through a sensible realm a rational ideal force is working out its own ultimate manifestation. These inferences were extended to nature: (a) She does nothing in vain; but all for an ulterior purpose. (b) Within natural sensible events there is therefore contained a spiritual causal force, which as spiritual escapes perception, but is apprehended by an enlightened reason. (c) The manifestation of this principle brings about a subordination of matter and sense to its own realization, and this ultimate fulfilment is the goal of nature and of man. The design argument thus operated in two directions. Purposefulness accounted for the intelligibility of nature and the possibility of science, while the absolute or cosmic character of this purposefulness gave sanction and worth to the moral and religious endeavors of man. Science was underpinned and morals authorized by one and the same principle, and their mutual agreement was eternally guaranteed.

This philosophy remained, in spite of sceptical and polemic outbursts, the official and the regnant philosophy of Europe for over two thousand years. The expulsion of fixed first and final causes from astronomy, physics, and chemistry had indeed given the doctrine something of a shock. But, on the other hand, increased acquaintance with the details of plant and animal life operated as a counterbalance and perhaps even strengthened the argument from design. The marvelous adaptations of organisms to their environment, of organs to the organism, of unlike parts of a complex organ—like the eye—to the organ itself; the foreshadowing by lower forms of the higher; the preparation in earlier stages of growth for organs that only later had their functioning—these things were increasingly recognized with the progress of botany, zoology, paleontology, and embryology. Together, they added such prestige to the design argument that by the late eighteenth century it was, as approved by the sciences of organic life, the central point of theistic and idealistic philosophy.

The Darwinian principle of natural selection cut straight under this philosophy. If all organic adaptations are due simply to constant variation and the elimination of those variations which are harmful in the struggle for existence that is brought about by excessive reproduction, there is no call for a prior intelligent causal force to plan and preordain them. Hostile critics charged Darwin with materialism and with making chance the cause of the universe. Some naturalists, like Asa Gray, favored the Darwinian principle and attempted to reconcile it with design. Gray held to what may be called design on the installment plan. If we conceive the "stream of variations" to be itself intended, we may suppose that each successive variation was designed from the first to be selected. In that case, variation, struggle, and selection simply define the mechanism of "secondary causes" through which the "first cause" acts; and the doctrine of design is none the worse off because we know more of its *modus operandi*. Darwin could not accept this mediating proposal. He admits or rather he asserts that it is "impossible to conceive this immense and wonderful universe including man with his capacity of looking far backwards and far into futurity as the result of blind chance or necessity." . . .

So much for some of the more obvious facts of the discussion of design *versus* chance, as causal principles of nature and of life as a whole. We brought up this discussion, you recall, as a crucial instance. What does our touchstone indicate as to the bearing of Darwinian ideas upon philosophy? In the first place, the new logic outlaws, flanks, dismisses—what you will—one type of problems and substitutes for it another type. Philosophy forswears inquiry after absolute origins and absolute finalities in order to explore specific values and the specific conditions that generate them.

Darwin concluded that the impossibility of assigning the world to chance as a whole and to design in its parts indicated the insolubility of the question. Two radically different reasons, however, may be given as to why a problem is insoluble. One reason is that the problem is too high for intelligence; the other is that the question in its very asking makes assumptions that render the question meaningless. The latter alternative is unerringly pointed to in the celebrated case of design *versus* chance. Once admit that the sole verifiable or fruitful object of knowledge is the particular set of changes that generate the object of study together with the consequences that then flow from it, and no intelligible question can be asked about what, by assumption, lies outside. To assert—as is often asserted—that specific values of particular truth, social bonds and forms of beauty, if they can be shown to be generated by concretely knowable conditions, are meaningless and in vain; to assert that they are justified only when they and their particular causes and effects have all at once been gathered up into some inclusive first cause and some exhaustive final goal, is intellectual atavism. Such argumentation is reversion to the logic that explained the extinction of fire by water through the formal essence of aqueousness and the quenching of thirst by water through the final cause of aqueousness. Whether used in the case of the special event or that of life as a whole, such logic only abstracts some aspect of the existing course of events in order to reduplicate it as a petrified eternal principle by which to explain the very changes of which it is the formalization.

When Henry Sidgwick* casually remarked in a letter that as he grew older his interest in what or who made the world was altered into interest in what kind of a world it is anyway, his voicing of a common experience of our own day illustrates also the nature of that intellectual transformation effected by the Darwinian logic. Interest shifts from the wholesale essence back of special changes to the question of how special changes serve and defeat concrete purposes; shifts from an intelligence that shaped things once for all to the particular intelligences which things are even now shaping; shifts from an ultimate goal of good to the direct increments of justice and happiness that intelligent administration of existent conditions may beget and that present carelessness or stupidity will destroy or forego.

In the second place, the classic type of logic inevitably set philosophy upon proving that life *must* have certain qualities and values—no matter how experience presents the matter—because of some remote cause and eventual goal. The duty of wholesale justification inevitably accompanies all thinking that makes the meaning of special occurrences depend upon something that once and for all lies behind them. The habit of derogating present meanings and uses prevents our looking the facts of experience in the face; it prevents serious acknowledgment of the evils they present and serious concern with the goods they promise but do not as yet fulfil. It turns thought to the business of finding a wholesale transcendent remedy for the one and guarantees for the other. One is reminded of the way many moralists and theologians greeted Herbert Spencer's recognition of an unknowable energy from which welled up the phenomenal physical processes without and the conscious operations within. Merely because Spencer labeled his unknowable energy "God," this faded piece of metaphysical goods was greeted as an important and grateful concession to the reality of the spiritual realm. Were it not for the deep hold of the habit of seeking justification for ideal values in the remote and transcendent, surely this

---

*[Editor's note: Henry Sidgwick (1838–1900) was an English economist and philosopher.]

reference of them to an unknowable absolute would be despised in comparison with the demonstrations of experience that knowable energies are daily generating about us precious values.

The displacing of this wholesale type of philosophy will doubtless not arrive by sheer logical disproof, but rather by growing recognition of its futility. Were it a thousand times true that opium produces sleep because of its dormitive energy, yet the inducing sleep in the tired, and the recovery to waking life of the poisoned, would not be thereby one least step forwarded. And were it a thousand times dialectically demonstrated that life as a whole is regulated by a transcendent principle to a final inclusive goal, none the less truth and error, health and disease, good and evil, hope and fear in the concrete, would remain just what and where they now are. To improve our education, to ameliorate our manners, to advance our politics, we must have recourse to specific conditions of generation.

Finally, the new logic introduces responsibility into the intellectual life. To idealize and rationalize the universe at large is after all a confession of inability to master the courses of things that specifically concern us. As long as mankind suffered from this impotency, it naturally shifted a burden of responsibility that it could not carry over to the more competent shoulders of the transcendent cause. But if insight into specific conditions of value and into specific consequences of ideas is possible, philosophy must in time become a method of locating and interpreting the more serious of the conflicts that occur in life, and a method of projecting ways for dealing with them: a method of moral and political diagnosis and prognosis.

The claim to formulate *a priori* the legislative constitution of the universe is by its nature a claim that may lead to elaborate dialectic developments. But it is also one that removes these very conclusions from subjection to experimental test, for, by definition, these results make no differences in the detailed course of events. But a philosophy that humbles its pretensions to the work of projecting hypotheses for the education and conduct of mind, individual and social, is thereby subjected to test by the way in which the ideas it propounds work out in practice. In having modesty forced upon it, philosophy also acquires responsibility.

Doubtless I seem to have violated the implied promise of my earlier remarks and to have turned both prophet and partisan. But in anticipating the direction of the transformations in philosophy to be wrought by the Darwinian genetic and experimental logic, I do not profess to speak for any save those who yield themselves consciously or unconsciously to this logic. No one can fairly deny that at present there are two effects of the Darwinian mode of thinking. On the one hand, there are making many sincere and vital efforts to revise our traditional philosophic conceptions in accordance with its demands. On the other hand, there is as definitely a recrudescence of absolutistic philosophies; an assertion of a type of philosophic knowing distinct from that of the sciences, one which opens to us another kind of reality from that to which the sciences give access; an appeal through experience to something that essentially goes beyond experience. This reaction affects popular creeds and religious movements as well as technical philosophies. The very conquest of the biological sciences by the new ideas has led many to proclaim an explicit and rigid separation of philosophy from science.

Old ideas give way slowly; for they are more than abstract logical forms and categories. They are habits, predispositions, deeply engrained attitudes of aversion and preference. Moreover, the conviction persists—though history shows it to be a hallucination—that all the questions that the human mind has asked are questions that can be answered in terms of the alternatives that the questions themselves present. But in fact intellectual progress usually occurs through sheer abandonment of questions together with both of the alternatives they assume—an abandonment that results from their decreasing vitality and a change of urgent interest. We do not solve them: we get over them. Old questions are solved by disappearing, evaporating, while new questions corresponding to the changed attitude of endeavor and preference take their place. Doubtless the greatest dissolvent in contemporary thought of old questions, the greatest precipitant of new methods, new intentions, new problems, is the one effected by the scientific revolution that found its climax in the *Origin of Species*.

A NOTE ON THE TYPE

The text of this book was set 10/12 Palatino using a film version of the face designed by Hermann Zapf that was first released in 1950 by Germany's Stempel Foundry. The face is named after Giovanni Battista Palatino, a famous penman of the sixteenth century. In its calligraphic quality, Palatino is reminiscent of the Italian Renaissance type designs, yet with its wide, open letters and unique proportions it still retains a modern feel. Palatino is considered one of the most important faces from one of Europe's most influential type designers.

Composed by Superior Type

Printed and bound by Arcata Graphics/Kingsport

About the Editor

R. Jackson Wilson is a Professor of History at Smith College, where he also teaches American studies and philosophy. His special field of interest is cultural history. His books include *In Quest of Community: Social Philosophy in the United States* and *Figures of Speech: American Writers and the Literary Marketplace, from Benjamin Franklin to Emily Dickinson.* He has taught at an unusually wide range of institutions, including the University of Wisconsin, the University of Arizona, Columbia University, Yale University, Hartford College for Women, the University of Massachusetts, Amherst College, Teacher's College (Columbia), and the Flinders University of South Australia.

AMERICAN SOCIETY AND CULTURE: THE DORSEY COLLECTION

AVAILABLE OR FORTHCOMING

SEX, DIET, AND DEBILITY IN JACKSONIAN AMERICA
Stephen Nissenbaum *University of Massachusetts*

INDUSTRIALIZATION AND SOUTHERN SOCIETY
James Cobb *University of Mississippi*

GARBAGE IN THE CITIES: REFUSE, REFORM, AND THE ENVIRONMENT
Martin Melosi *University of Houston*

THE TRANS–APPALACHIAN FRONTIER
Malcolm J. Rohrbough *University of Iowa*

THE LAND OFFICE BUSINESS
Malcolm J. Rohrbough *University of Iowa*

SLUM AND GHETTO
Thomas J. Philpott *University of Texas*

THE UNEMBARRASSED MUSE
Russel B. Nye, *Emeritus* *Michigan State University*

THE WIZARD OF OZ
L. Frank Baum
Introduction by William R. Leach *New York University*

THE SOULS OF BLACK FOLK
W. E. B. Du Bois
Introduction by David L. Lewis *Rutgers University*